WASHINGTON'S
MONUMENT

Overlanding:
How to Explore the World on Four Wheels

The Scarlet Woman of Wall Street:
Jay Gould, Jim Fisk, Cornelius Vanderbilt,
and the Erie Railway Wars

Hamilton's Blessing:
The Extraordinary Life and Times of Our National Debt

The Great Game:
The Emergence of Wall Street as a World Power: 1653–2000

The Business of America:
Tales from the Marketplace—American Enterprise from the
Settling of New England to the Breakup of AT&T

A Thread Across the Ocean:
The Heroic Story of the Transatlantic Cable

An Empire of Wealth:
The Epic History of American Economic Power

WASHINGTON'S
MONUMENT

And the Fascinating History of the Obelisk

JOHN STEELE GORDON

B L O O M S B U R Y

NEW YORK · LONDON · OXFORD · NEW DELHI · SYDNEY

Bloomsbury USA
An imprint of Bloomsbury Publishing Plc

1385 Broadway	50 Bedford Square
New York	London
NY 10018	WC1B 3DP
USA	UK

www.bloomsbury.com

BLOOMSBURY and the Diana logo are trademarks of Bloomsbury Publishing Plc

First published 2016

ISBN: HB: 978-1-62040-650-2
          ePub: 978-1-62040-652-6

Library of Congress Cataloging-in-Publication Data

Names: Gordon, John Steele, author.
Title: Washington's monument : and the fascinating history of the obelisk / John Steele Gordon.
Description: New York : Bloomsbury USA, 2016.
Identifiers: LCCN 2015036462 | ISBN 9781620406502 (hardback)
Subjects: LCSH: Washington Monument (Washington, D.C.)—History. | Washington, George, 1732-1799—Monuments—Washington (D.C.) | Washington (D.C.)—Buildings, structures, etc. | BISAC: HISTORY / United States / General. | ARCHITECTURE / Buildings / Landmarks & Monuments.
Classification: LCC F203.4.W3 G67 2016 | DDC 975.3—dc23 LC record available at http://lccn.loc.gov/2015036462

2 4 6 8 10 9 7 5 3 1

Typeset by RefineCatch Limited, Bungay, Suffolk
Printed and bound in USA by Berryville Graphics Inc., Berryville, Virginia

To
"The East Room Gang"

So as regards these two great obelisks
Wrought with electrum by my majesty for my father Amun
In order that my name may endure in this temple
For eternity and everlastingness
They are each made of one block of hard granite
Without seam, without joining together

—INSCRIPTION ON THE BASE OF AN OBELISK
RAISED BY THE PHARAOH HATSHEPSUT

The obelisk is not an arbitrary structure, . . . Its objects, forms and proportions were fixed by the usage of thousands of years; they satisfy every cultivated eye, and I hold it an esthetical crime to depart from them.

—GEORGE PERKINS MARSH

It seems to be a peculiarity . . . of operations with obelisks that unforeseen hitches will occur and cause delay.

—LIEUTENANT SEATON SCHROEDER, USN

Every object in a state of uniform motion tends to remain in that state of motion unless an external force is applied to it.

—SIR ISAAC NEWTON

CONTENTS

CONTENTS

A Fascinating Shape

AT 1:51 IN the afternoon of August 23, 2011, the ground beneath Washington, D.C., began to move. People fled from buildings, trains halted, objects fell off shelves, roads cracked. It was not a killer earthquake, but at 5.8 on the Richter scale, it was the most powerful earthquake east of the Mississippi since 1944 and it did considerable damage.

Among the casualties was one of the capital's most famous structures, the Washington Monument. Except for its elevator shaft and stairway, the monument is constructed entirely of stone, more than thirty-six thousand separate blocks. And stone structures are highly intolerant of earthquakes. Unlike wooden and steel buildings, they cannot flex as the seismic waves pass through the earth, shaking everything above. Instead, stone structures crack. Making matters worse, the Washington Monument is an obelisk, ten times as tall as it is wide at the base and weighing fully 90,854 tons and thus more vulnerable than wider, squatter buildings.

And crack it did. The most heavily damaged part was the pyramidion, the pyramid shape at the top, where many of the stones cracked or had pieces chipped off. But damage was done to the entire structure, especially at the corners. Much mortar between the massive stone blocks was lost. Daylight coming through the cracks could be seen from the inside in some places.

Earthquake damage to the Washington Monument, August 23, 2011.

While the monument came nowhere close to falling down, it was in need of serious repair, for otherwise water would be able to penetrate into the structure and eventually destroy it. Before one of the capital's most iconic structures was again open to the public, the repairs would cost fifteen million dollars and take nearly three years.*

WASHINGTON WITHOUT THE Washington Monument is almost unimaginable today. The tallest structure, by law, in the city, it is visible from all parts of the metropolis. The view from the top is spectacular, which is one reason it has six hundred thousand visitors a year.

And while the Capitol Building symbolizes Congress and the American nation, and the White House the presidency, the Washington Monument has come to symbolize the city itself, much as Big Ben symbolizes London and the Eiffel Tower Paris. Like those two iconic structures, the monument is tall and dominates its surroundings. But it is far simpler in design, and any child, however untalented, could draw a picture of it. Its power comes as much from its simplicity as from its size.

Like all obelisks, the monument is merely four identical sides, each a greatly elongated trapezoid, capped with

---

* The gothic-style Washington National Cathedral, another stone structure, was even more heavily damaged in the earthquake, with finials toppled and flying buttresses cracked. Fortunately, the stone vaulting held and so the roof remained intact. Unfortunately, it was not insured for earthquake damage—no one thought that a likely possibility in Washington—and so the $26 million estimated cost of repairs is being raised privately.

The Washington Monument today.

a four-sided pyramid, whose sides slope at a seventy-three-degree angle from the horizontal. It soars more than 555 feet into the sky, the tallest stone structure on earth and, by far, the largest obelisk, its white marble facing gleaming on sunny days.

The Washington Monument has always been the odd man out of the capital city of the United States. Most of the major buildings, such as the Capitol, the White House, the Treasury, the Lincoln and Jefferson memorials, and the Supreme Court, were inspired by Roman and Greek architectural models. Other major buildings, such as the Eisenhower Executive Office Building west of the White House, the original Smithsonian Institution building, the Pentagon, the State Department, and the Kennedy Center, were designed in the architectural (and bureaucratic) fashions of their own day.

But the Washington Monument has architectural roots that vastly predate even the glory that was Greece and the grandeur that was Rome, let alone the Victorian age that saw its erection. It is, instead, modeled on a style of monument that was perfected in ancient Egypt during the period known as the New Kingdom (circa 1550–1077 B.C.), when Egyptian power reached its zenith under such pharaohs as Thutmose III and Rameses II.

The Egyptian obelisks that now adorn such cities as Rome, Istanbul, Paris, London, and New York all date from the height of the New Kingdom. But it is a bit hard to grasp just how ancient they are. As Seaton Schroeder, the assistant engineer in charge of bringing the New York obelisk to Central Park in 1881, wrote in an appendix to the book by Henry Gorringe, the chief engineer of that project,

> This mighty monument of hoary antiquity is an
> enduring tablet whereon the hierologist may decipher

the secrets of a remoter past. From the carvings on its face we read of an age anterior to most events recorded in ancient history; Troy had not fallen, Homer was not born, Solomon's temple was not built; and Rome arose, conquered the world, and passed into history during the time that this austere chronicle of silent ages has braved the elements.

Unlike the other presidential memorials in Washington, the centerpiece of the Washington Monument is the monument itself, not the statue of the man honored. Daniel Chester French's magnificent, oversize statue of the seated Abraham Lincoln dominates the building that houses it and Thomas Jefferson's bronze statue is the centerpiece of his memorial. But the statue of George Washington in his monument is in an inconspicuous niche on the ground floor and receives little attention. Indeed, it was very much an afterthought, placed there only in 1994, more than a century after the monument's completion. It is the monument itself that people come to visit.

And in a city that values symmetry, while it is on the axis running between the Capitol and the Lincoln Memorial, the monument is a few hundred yards east of the axis between the White House and the Jefferson Memorial. It thus misses being in the crossing of the cruciform design of ceremonial Washington.

Perhaps most curious of all, it is utterly devoid of ornament, the very antithesis of the architectural fashion of

Statue of George Washington inside the Monument bearing his name.

the high Victorian years during which it was constructed, between 1848 and 1884. But that was more by accident than by design.

Because the monument was to be privately funded, by donations from across the country, the project took nearly forty years to complete. And it was completed even then only because Congress finally put up the funds to do so. There was never enough money to build the original concept, which had an elaborate pantheon at the base to honor both Washington and the other Founding Fathers. Nor were later suggestions, such as turning it into a gothic tower, financially practicable.

So the Washington Monument is proof that sometimes just muddling through produces superior results.

When Congress appropriated money, in 1876, to finish the monument, the chief engineer was influenced at the critical moment by the American minister to the newly created Kingdom of Italy, who measured the proportions of the Egyptian obelisks that are found in profusion in the squares of Rome. He convinced the engineer to make the Washington Monument conform exactly to those ancient proportions and to the severe simplicity of design characteristic of true Egyptian obelisks.*

The result was an obelisk that, even today, is more than twice the height of any other on earth and can be seen from almost every neighborhood of the District of Columbia.

But the Washington Monument is no less powerful for being odd. The reason, undoubtedly, is its shape, one that has fascinated Egyptians, who carved and erected them; Roman emperors, who stole them; popes, who placed one before Saint Peter's Basilica at the very heart of Catholicism; and generals, presidents, and robber barons, who are buried beneath them. The cemeteries where the prosperous of the Victorian age were laid to rest, such as Green-Wood Cemetery in Brooklyn and Woodlawn in the Bronx, fairly bristle with obelisks. Battlefields, such as Bunker Hill, Saratoga, Bennington, and San Jacinto, are marked by them.

The beginning point of the Public Land Survey of the United States, from which three fourths of the continental

---

* A true obelisk is a monolith, i.e., carved from a single piece of stone (which is what *monolith* means in Greek). The Washington Monument, made of granite blocks faced with marble, is, technically at least, only obelisk shaped.

United States was eventually mapped, is marked near East Liverpool, Ohio, by an obelisk, although, to be sure, it is a distinctly squat one, erected in 1881.

The obelisk, silent as only stone can be, nonetheless seems to say as nothing else can, "Here is something significant."

NOT THE LEAST of the obelisk's history is the extraordinary engineering required to create, move, erect, lower,

The Bunker Hill Monument in Charlestown, Massachusetts, memorializing the historic battle during the American Revolution.

and re-erect them through the ages. Thus the history of the obelisk is a window into engineering technologies over time.

The ancient Egyptians lacked even iron tools, let alone steam engines, hydraulic jacks, capstans, and compound pulleys. Their successors, the Romans, Renaissance popes, and status-seeking nations of the nineteenth century, had more and more tools available. But building and erecting an obelisk was always a very difficult job, with no guarantee of success and a terrible price to pay for failure.

Engineers of great skill—and great daring—all had to deal, in their own ways, with the obelisk's most overwhelming physical attribute, which is inertia: the tendency of objects to remain in a state of rest or motion unless acted upon by an outside force. The greater the mass of the object, the greater the force needed to change its inertial state. Mustering and controlling those outside forces in order to get these immense, concentrated weights both to move and—equally important—to stop on command, making use of the technology available at the time, was the task these engineers had to deal with.

THE FASCINATING STORY of the obelisk involves pharaohs, emperors, mathematicians, apostles, popes, engineers, philologists, ship captains, naval architects, lawyers, newspaper editors, politicians, priests, Masons, millionaires, Know-Nothings, and even the fathers of the sciences of ecology and oceanography.

And behind all of them were the countless thousands, forever unknown to history, whose muscle power, not to mention blood, toil, tears, and sweat, made the obelisk possible.

CHAPTER ONE

The Father of His Country

THE ORIGINS OF the Washington Monument go all the way back to August 7, 1783, even before the signing of the Treaty of Paris—the treaty in which Britain recognized American independence.* With victory well within sight, however, the Continental Congress wanted to honor the man who more than any other had made that independence possible. To do so, Congress resolved "that an equestrian

---

* The treaty was finally signed on September 3, 1783, nearly two years after British general Lord Cornwallis's defeat at Yorktown ended the military phase of the conflict. But, because transatlantic travel was so slow in the eighteenth century—a westbound voyage could easily take two months—Congress did not ratify the treaty until January 14, 1784. Britain then ratified it on April 9, and the ratifications were exchanged on May 12. It would be well into summer 1784 before that news, and the ratified treaty, reached the United States. It is today in the National Archives.

statue of General Washington be erected at the place where the residence of Congress shall be established. . . . the statue should be supported by a marble pedestal on which should be represented four principal events of the war in which he commanded in person."

On the base Congress ordered the following inscription: "The United States, in Congress assembled, ordered this statue to be erected in the year of our Lord, 1783, in honor of George Washington, the illustrious Commander-in-Chief of the Armies of the United States of America during the war which vindicated and secured their liberty, sovereignty, and independence."

Even then, when Washington was only fifty-one, he was recognized as one of the great men of history, and not just in this country. While having his portrait painted by the American-born Benjamin West that year, King George III asked the painter what Washington planned to do once peace was achieved. West told the king that Washington intended to resign his commission and retire to his estate at Mount Vernon. "If he does that," said the astounded monarch, "he will be the greatest man in the world."

Thirty years later, Lord Byron wrote on the fall of Napoleon,

> *Where may the wearied eye repose*
> *When gazing on the Great;*
> *Where neither guilty glory glows,*
> *Nor despicable state?*

Yes—one—the first—the last—the best—
The Cincinnatus of the West,
Whom envy dared not hate,
Bequeathed the name of Washington,
To make man blush there was but one!

But while Washington's greatness was already manifest and Congress's gratitude genuine, the newly independent United States was bankrupt. There was no money for the everyday concerns of government, or even to pay interest or principal on the debt, let alone to pay for monumental statues. It would remain no more than a congressional resolution for many years. In fact, more than a hundred years would pass before a monument to the father of his country was completed in that country's capital.*

WASHINGTON INDEED RESIGNED his commission in the army and retired to Mount Vernon to happily take up again the life of a country gentleman. But that did not last long. The fiscal situation of the government went from bad to worse. The Articles of Confederation, which had been signed by Congress in 1777 and had taken effect in 1781, had

---

* The first monument to Washington in the country was erected in 1827 on South Mountain, near Boonsboro, Maryland. On July 4 of that year, the town's citizens assembled in the town square at seven A.M. and marched to the site, where they laid the base and built a tower to the height of fifteen feet. Later that year, it was completed to a height of thirty feet. It is still there, in what is now Washington Monument State Park.

The first monument to George Washington, erected in 1827, near Boonsboro, Maryland.

produced a singularly weak central government, not altogether unlike today's United Nations.

Members of Congress were appointed by the state legislatures and, much as UN delegates are responsible to their own countries, were responsible to their states, bound to follow their state governments' instructions. Worse, the confederation government had no independent power to tax. Instead, again like the UN, Congress had to requisition money from the various state governments. Sometimes the state governments paid and, beset with their own fiscal woes, sometimes they did not.

By the late 1780s, the situation had reached a crisis point and delegates assembled in Philadelphia in the summer of 1787, supposedly to amend the Articles of Confederation. Instead they quickly decided to exceed their instructions and write a whole new constitution. George Washington, one of the delegates, was soon elected president of the convention. Two years later, the constitution having been ratified by twelve of the thirteen states, he was unanimously elected president of the country.*

For eight years Washington led the new federal government, with little to guide him but common sense. Fortunately he was richly endowed with that quality. As he explained, "I walk on untrodden ground. There is scarcely any part of my conduct which may not hereafter be drawn into precedent." For instance, when the question came up in the Senate of how to address the president, Vice President John Adams, sitting as president of the Senate, suggested "Your Highness." Washington chose the plain, republican "Mr. President" instead.

Toward the end of his second term he declined to run again, setting still another precedent. Washington had received much more criticism in his second term, as American politics began to divide into parties. Washington had become identified as a Federalist, the party philosophically spearheaded by Alexander Hamilton. The followers of Thomas Jefferson, who called themselves the Democratic-Republicans, often savaged Washington in the fiercely partisan, party-dominated press of the day.

---

* Rhode Island, which had a thriving smuggling industry and thus did not like the idea of federal control of imports and exports, did not ratify until May 1790.

Still, when Washington died on December 14, 1799, not many Americans disagreed with Light-Horse Harry Lee when, in his eulogy, he called Washington "first in war, first in peace, first in the hearts of his countrymen."

Almost immediately a movement arose to revive the idea of a monument in Washington's honor. Just ten days after his death Representative John Marshall, who less than two years later would be named chief justice, offered a motion in the House "that a marble monument be erected by the United States at the City of Washington, and that the family of General Washington be requested to permit his body to be deposited under it; and that the monument be so designed as to commemorate the great events of his military and political life." Martha Washington agreed to allow his body to be reinterred under the proposed memorial.*

At first, Congress proposed to carry out the plan for the equestrian statue that Congress had authorized in 1783. But that soon changed to a "mausoleum of American granite and marble, in pyramidal form, one hundred feet square at the base and of a proportionate height." At the same base-to-height ratio as the Great Pyramid at Giza, Washington's pyramid would have been a little over sixty-three feet tall.

But, again, the proposal went nowhere, as the Senate did not act. On March 4, 1801, with the inauguration of Thomas Jefferson, the Democratic-Republicans took

---

* Marshall was a great admirer of Washington and between 1804 and 1807, while sitting as chief justice, he would write a five-volume *Life of Washington*. It is still in print.

control of both houses of Congress and the White House and were not inclined to build a monument to the nation's first president, whom they had come to regard as a political opponent.

The idea would be revived again and again, including by President John Quincy Adams in his first annual message to Congress in December 1825.* But only as the centennial of Washington's birth approached in 1832 did the idea of a monument begin to get serious consideration. By that time the political quarrels of a generation earlier had been forgotten and Washington had become what he has been ever since, simply the Father of his Country.

The last of several attempts to have Washington's body removed from Mount Vernon to be deposited in the crypt of the Capitol Building failed that year when John Augustine Washington, then the owner of Mount Vernon, refused permission. But Congress did authorize a large statue of Washington to be created by the American sculptor Horatio Greenough, to be placed in the rotunda of the Capitol.

When the statue was finished, in 1841, it immediately created considerable controversy. Larger than life size, it was modeled on Phidias's statue of Zeus Olympios, one of the seven wonders of the ancient world. It depicted

---

* Adams only delivered a copy to Congress. Thomas Jefferson, a poor and reluctant public speaker, had stopped the practice of giving the State of the Union speech before a joint session and just sent it in in written form. Not until Woodrow Wilson, an excellent public speaker, did the practice of addressing Congress directly resume. Only then did it become a great state occasion.

a seated Washington, naked to the waist, wearing a toga and sandals, his right hand pointing toward heaven and his left holding a sheathed sword, hilt outward, symbolizing the surrender of his commission after the Revolutionary War.

Many thought a half-naked Washington was either offensive or funny. It was soon removed from the rotunda and then had a rather peripatetic existence. Banished to the east lawn of the Capitol in 1843, it was later moved to a site outside the Patent Office. In 1908 it was moved to the Smithsonian Castle on the National Mall and in 1964 to what is now the National Museum of American History, where it can be seen today.

Horatio Greenough's statue of George Washington modeled on Phidias's statue of Zeus.

Fed up with Congressional dithering, prominent Washingtonians began to organize to build "a great National Monument to the memory of Washington at the seat of the Federal Government." In September 1833, the *Daily National Intelligencer*, the leading Washington newspaper of the day, announced a public meeting to be held in the aldermen's chamber of Washington's City Hall on September 26. There those in attendance decided to form the Washington National Monument Society to raise funds and design a suitable memorial.

The first president of the society was Chief Justice John Marshall, then seventy-eight years old. He was expected to serve as a figurehead with the real work to be done by the first vice president, Judge William Cranch. The second official "Reporter of Decisions" of the Supreme Court, Cranch is famous, as a judge, for his judicial slap down of a defendant who argued that being drunk lessened his responsibility for his crime. "It often happens," Cranch wrote, "that the prisoner seeks to palliate his crime by the pleas of intoxication; as if the voluntary abandonment of reason . . . were not, of itself, an offense sufficient to make him responsible for all of its consequences." He was also the great grandfather of the poet T. S. Eliot.

Marshall replied to Cranch's letter informing him of his election:

> *I received yesterday your letter of the 22d, informing me that the "Washington Monument Society" has done me the honor to choose me as its President.*

John Marshall, first president of the Washington National Monument
Society.

*You are right in supposing that the most ardent wish
of my heart is to see some lasting testimonial of the grateful
affection of his country erected to the memory of her first
citizen. I have always wished it, and have always thought
that the Metropolis of the Union was the fit place for this
National Monument. I cannot, therefore, refuse to take
any place which the Society may assign me; and though
my advanced age forbids the hope of being useful, I am
encouraged by the name of the First Vice-President to
believe that in him ample compensation will be found for
any defects in the President.*

Marshall would serve until his death on July 6, 1835, and he was succeeded by former president James Madison.* When Madison himself died less than a year later, the society decided to make the president of the United States the ex officio president of the society.

The society sent out notices asking people to donate and fulfill the unfulfilled promise of Congress. To make the fund-raising as democratic as possible, individual contributions were limited to no more than a dollar a year.† Funds came in very slowly and by 1836 only twenty-eight thousand dollars had been raised. They slowed to a trickle the next year as the great depression of 1837–43 began. But if the society lacked the funds to build a monument, it could at least design one. It placed advertisements in newspapers soliciting designs and specified only that the proposed structure "harmoniously blend durability, simplicity, and grandeur." It expected that construction costs would exceed one million dollars.

Many designs were submitted, but the winner was from Robert Mills (1781–1855), one of the country's first native-born, professionally trained architects. Born in Charleston, South Carolina, he studied at the College of Charleston and then moved to Philadelphia, where he studied under Benjamin Latrobe, who had trained as an

---

* Marshall was still serving as Chief Justice at the time of his death, having served longer than any Chief Justice before or since.

† That doesn't sound like much to modern ears, but in the 1830s you could buy lunch for a nickel and for much of the nineteenth century a dollar a day was a standard wage for unskilled work.

Architect Robert Mills, original designer of the Washington Monument.

architect in his native England. In 1803, Thomas Jefferson appointed Latrobe surveyor of the public buildings of the United States, in which capacity Latrobe would supervise the ongoing construction of the new Capitol Building in Washington.

Mills also studied under the Irish-born James Hoban, the architect of the White House. He soon made the acquaintance of Thomas Jefferson, no mean architect himself. Mills's practice flourished and he built many prominent buildings in Philadelphia, Baltimore, Washington, and South Carolina. Among his best-known Washington buildings are the Treasury Building, east of the White House, and the Old Patent Office Building that now houses the National Portrait Gallery and the Smithsonian American Art Museum.*

Mills's design for the Washington Monument called for a vast circular colonnaded building, 250 feet in diameter and 100 feet high, above which would tower an obelisk, 50 feet square at the base and rising to a total height of 600 feet. It was to be surmounted by a star, "emblematic of the glory which the name of Washington has attained." At the base, Mills called for a great statue of Washington along with statues of the signers of the Declaration of Independence, and Washington's tomb.

While the society chose Mills's design, it never formally accepted the colonnade and its elaborate interior and subterranean halls. In any event, as a matter of construction, it could not be built until the obelisk itself was finished. Money problems prevented it from being built at all.

Of course, the society needed a site and that meant petitioning Congress. In 1838 it did so, asking for a site on the Mall, which at that time existed far more on Pierre L'Enfant's original plan for Washington, D.C., than in reality. Indeed, most of what is now the western half of the Mall was then under the waters of the Potomac River. On June 15, a bill was presented in the Senate but ran into considerable criticism. Noting that the society had reported

---

* Both buildings have been greatly enlarged since Mills's day but have remained faithful to his original designs.

Original design for the Washington Monument.

receiving about thirty thousand dollars in contributions and interest at that point, Senator William Allen, Democrat of Ohio, said that he believed the society had collected more than that just in his own state.*

Appalled to be, in effect, accused of running a scam, the society sent the Senate a memorial. "The Board of Managers of the Washington National Monument Society, having seen in the public prints a statement that representations have been made in your body derogatory to their character, consider it their duty to lay before you an official account of their receipts and expenditures."

The memorial showed that Ohio had contributed $6,391.19, the most of any state, while Vermont had contributed a paltry $31.95. Nonetheless, the Senate decided to table the bill, fearing that since the monument was to stand on federal land, if the society ran out of money, the government would have no choice but to pay for its completion.†

To help raise money, the society had lithographs made of the proposed design to be given to those who contributed at least one dollar, and the restriction on contributions to that amount was rescinded. At the bottom, with the

---

* William Allen was known for his remarkably loud voice, a great asset to a politician at that time. Asked if someone was still in Washington, Allen's fellow Ohio senator, Benjamin Tappan, replied that he was not, "but if you will go to Bill Allen and tell him to raise that window and call him he will come back." Allen's statue has been in Statuary Hall in the Capitol since 1887, but it is scheduled to be replaced by one of a far more consequential Ohioan, Thomas Edison, as soon as the money is raised.

† In that respect, the Senate was entirely correct, although it would only appropriate money almost forty years later.

words, "Earnestly recommended to the favor of our countrymen," it was signed by many of the major politicians of
the day, among them Zachary Taylor, Millard Fillmore,
James K. Polk, John Quincy Adams, Daniel Webster,
Henry Clay, and George M. Dallas, who would be vice
president under Polk.

But only when the depression began to lift in 1843
did the pace of contributions begin to quicken and with
it, the hope that the project could, at last, get under way.
By the mid-1840s, after fifteen years of effort, the Washington Monument appeared ready to become a reality at
last. By 1847, the society had raised eighty-seven thousand
dollars, which was thought enough to at least begin
construction.

On January 31, 1848, Congress passed a resolution that
authorized "a Monument to the memory of George Washington upon such portion of the public grounds or reserva-
tions within the City of Washington, not otherwise
occupied, as shall be selected by the President of the United
States and the Board of Managers of [the Washington
National Monument] Society as a suitable site on which to
erect the said Monument, and for the necessary protection
thereof."

The site was chosen for both practical and symbolic
reasons. "The site selected presents a beautiful view of the
Potomac," the society explained, "is so elevated that
the Monument will be seen from all parts of the city and
the surrounding country, and, being a public reservation,
it is safe from any future obstruction of the view. It is

so near the river that materials for constructing the Monument can be conveyed to it from the river at but little expense; stone, sand, and lime, all of the best kind, can be brought to it by water from convenient distances; and marble of the most beautiful quality, obtained at a distance of only eleven miles from Baltimore, on the Susquehanna Railroad, can be brought either on the railroad or in vessels."

Pierre L'Enfant had originally planned for a statue of Washington on the spot, directly south of the White House and due west of the Capitol, and Thomas Jefferson had placed a meridian marker there to mark what would be America's prime meridian.*

But while that spot was the obvious one, it was not ultimately deemed suitable because the high water table and soft earth made a proper foundation impossible with nineteenth-century technology, especially with a structure at once so heavy and with so small a footprint. (No one, surely, wanted an American Leaning Tower of Pisa.) The land three hundred fifty feet to the east was a bit higher and therefore drier and gave the monument more visibility from around the city.

A committee, consisting of Brigadier General Archibald Henderson, commandant of the Marine Corps; Lieutenant Matthew Fontaine Maury, superintendent of the United States Naval Observatory; and Walter Lenox,

---

* The world would not agree on everyone using the Greenwich meridian as the prime meridian until the 1880s.

Lt. Matthew Fontaine Maury.

president of the city's Board of Aldermen, was named to arrange for the laying of the cornerstone.*

They initially planned to lay the cornerstone on February 22, 1848, Washington's one hundred sixteenth birthday. But the time was too short and the ceremony was

---

* Archibald Henderson was commandant of the Marine Corps for a record 38 years, from 1820 until his sudden death in 1859. After marines served in the Battle of Chapultepec during the Mexican-American War, Henderson was presented with a sword inscribed "From the Halls of Montezuma to the Shores of Tripoli," which later became the opening line of the "Marines' Hymn."

Matthew Fontaine Maury was one of the great scientists of the nineteenth century, remembered as the father of oceanography. His book *The Physical Geography of the Sea,* published in 1855, was the first major work in the new science.

postponed until July 4 of that year. Thomas Symington of Baltimore quarried and presented to the society a block of marble weighing 24,500 pounds. It was cut for use as the cornerstone and dressed by Matthew G. Emery, a local builder and mason, who did not charge for the work. He also carved out a hole for a zinc box that held statistics on the city of Washington, coins and bills, a Bible, and sixty newspapers.*

The stone arrived in Washington by railroad and was transferred to a cart and slowly hauled to the site. But crossing a rickety bridge over the Washington Canal, which then ran about where Constitution Avenue is today, the cart broke through the bridge and landed in the mud. Forty workmen from the Washington Navy Yard came to help, along with some Marine Band musicians and a crowd of onlookers. They attached ropes to the cart and managed to free it from the mud. They then hauled it to the building site. Today the cornerstone is part of the monument's foundation and lies thirty-six feet beneath ground level, under the northeast corner.

Former president John Quincy Adams had been invited to deliver the oration, the centerpiece of every major Victorian ceremony, but he declined on account of health.†

---

* Matthew Emery would later be elected Mayor of Washington, just before the office itself was abolished by Congress in 1871. Washington would not have another mayor until 1975.

† Indeed, Adams suffered a massive stroke on February 21, 1848, on the floor of the House of Representatives, of which he was a member, the only ex-president to sit in Congress. He died two days later, in the Speaker's Room of the Capitol. His last words were, "This is the last of earth. I am content."

Senator Daniel Webster, one of the great orators of his time, also declined because of the press of business and the shortness of time. Eventually, the Speaker of the House, Robert C. Winthrop, accepted the assignment.*

As a contemporary newspaper account described it, "The day was fine. The rain had laid the dust and infused a delicious freshness in the air. The procession was extensive and beautiful. It embraced many military companies of our own and our sister cities—various associations, with their characteristic emblems; the President and Cabinet and various officers of the Executive Departments; many of the Members of Congress; citizens and strangers who had poured into the city." Mrs. Alexander Hamilton, then ninety-one years old, was there as was Dolley Madison, who was eighty.

A consecration prayer was offered, Speaker Winthrop delivered his "lofty and eloquent" oration, and then Benjamin B. French, Masonic Grand Master, delivered another address and presided over the Masonic ceremony for laying a cornerstone. He used the same gavel George Washington, himself a Mason, had used at the laying of the cornerstone of the Capitol Building on September 18, 1793. Finally, a song and a benediction ended the ceremony.

After sixty-five years, the building of a monument in the nation's capital to the man who had given his name to

---

* Winthrop is the great great grandfather of Secretary of State John Kerry.

that capital was finally under way. One suspects that few of the fifteen thousand to twenty thousand people who attended the ceremony imagined that another thirty-seven years would pass before it would be finished.

CHAPTER TWO

The Gift of the Nile

THE LAND WHERE the obelisk originated is the most
ancient nation on earth. About 3150 B.C., King Menes
unified the Upper and Lower Kingdoms and, despite civil
wars and foreign conquests, there has been an Egyptian
nation ever since.*

To get a grasp of just how long Egyptian history is,
consider that the last pharaoh, Cleopatra VII, the lover of
both Julius Caesar and Mark Antony, committed suicide
in 30 B.C., supposedly from the bite of an asp. That was

---

* Egypt would not be fully self-governing between 30 B.C. and A.D. 1922, as it was
successively parts of the Roman, Byzantine, Arab, Ottoman, and British empires.
But Egyptians never lost their sense of being Egyptian, whoever was calling the
shots at the top of the government.

2,046 years ago. Yet the Great Pyramid at Giza was built about 2560 B.C. In other words, Cleopatra is closer to us in time—by more than half a millennium—than she is to the Pharaoh Khufu (often called Cheops, the Hellenized form of his name) for whom the great pyramid was built.

Egypt's peculiar geography has allowed it to survive so long. Protected from land invasion by other civilized states by the hostile terrain of the Sinai Peninsula, Egyptians lived largely unmolested in the extraordinarily fertile Nile Valley. The Greek historian Herodotus, who wrote extensively (if perhaps not always very accurately) about Egypt in his *Histories*, described Egypt as "the gift of the Nile." Not only did the river supply abundant water in a very dry desert (Cairo gets less than an inch of rain per year), but it provided easy transportation for both people and goods. The river's annual flood would deposit another layer of rich soil on the fields, making Egypt the most agriculturally productive place in the ancient world. Exporting her large surpluses of wheat and other grains made her one of the richest.*

The Nile dominated ancient Egypt and both the country's annual cycle and quotidian routines were determined by the river. The cycle began in what we call early August, marked by both the heliacal rising of Sirius, the

---

* Because the Egyptians often had to survey the land after the flood, they became expert at the mathematics involved. Pythagoras may have first proved his famous theorem, but the Egyptians, thousands of years earlier, well understood that the angle opposite the longest side of a 3×4×5 triangle was a 90-degree angle. Such knowledge stood them in good stead when they began building on a grand scale.

brightest star in the sky, and a change in the color of the river's water.* Rain that had fallen thousands of miles to the south, in Ethiopia, had reached Egypt and the river began to rise.

The Egyptian year was divided into three seasons, known as the inundation, growth, and harvest. During the four months when the Nile was in flood, the peasantry of ancient Egypt was available as corvée labor to build the tombs, temples, and statues that still dominate the landscape.

With its wealth, isolation from other cultures, and relative peace, ancient Egypt developed a deeply conservative and idiosyncratic society. Indeed, so conservative was Egyptian art that only Egyptologists can tell whether a particular statue or wall painting dates to the third, second, or first millennium B.C. because styles in Egyptian art changed so little over that great time period. And because of Egypt's dry climate, much of its art has survived the ages.

But Egypt is most notable for its monumental architecture. The Great Pyramid is the only survivor among the seven wonders of the ancient world and was the world's tallest manmade structure from its completion until it was surpassed nearly four thousand years later by Lincoln Cathedral in England. The pyramid's base covers more than thirteen acres and it weighs 6, 500,000 tons, all of it hauled, lifted, and placed by human muscle power. Equally

---

* The heliacal rising of a star is when that star can first be seen after emerging from conjunction with the sun.

impressive, a statue of Rameses II that once stood in Tanis in lower Egypt had a big toe the size of a man's body. It must have stood about ninety-two feet high.*

Most monumental stonework was in the form of temples, such as the great temple complexes at Karnak and Heliopolis; tombs, such as the pyramids; or the huge statues of pharaohs. But the Egyptians also quarried and transported stone for obelisks, which they erected in great numbers. There are twenty-eight still standing, although only six of these are in Egypt, and many more are known to have existed in the past. Egyptians usually placed them in pairs on either side of temple entrances.

They were associated with the sun god, who was at the center of ancient Egypt's complex religion. Perhaps their shape was inspired by rays of sunlight; and the tops were often covered in gold or electrum (an amalgam of gold and silver) to catch the first rays of the dawning sun.

But while the obelisk is purely an Egyptian invention, the word itself is Greek. The English word comes from the Greek *obeliskos*, which means "little spit" or "skewer." The ancient Egyptian word for obelisk is *tekhen* (plural *tekhenu*), which derives from the word for "to pierce."†

---

* It was recycled by a later pharaoh who used the stone in a temple he was building, the fate of many ancient monuments, and not just in Egypt. The Colosseum in Rome was used as a quarry in the early Middle Ages. The Great Pyramid itself was stripped of its outer casing to provide stone for the building of Cairo.

† Many words for what are quintessentially Egyptian things, such as the pyramids, derive from Greek words, including even the word *Egypt* itself. *Pyramid* comes from the Greek word for honeycake, which was, apparently, pyramid shaped. *Hieroglyphic* comes from the Greek for "sacred writings."

While obelisks were very much a part of the Egyptian religion, and thus ultimately mysterious to us, at least once an obelisk helped greatly to advance science. The Greek philosopher and mathematician Eratosthenes (c. 276–c. 194 B.C.) lived much of his adult life in Alexandria, then the intellectual capital of the Mediterranean world, and was the head librarian of the great library at Alexandria.

Like all educated people in the ancient world, he knew that the earth was round, but he didn't know how far around it was. He had been told that at Syene, modern day Aswan, at noon on the day of the summer solstice, uprights cast no shadows and the sun shone down to the bottoms of wells. He also knew that on that day at Alexandria, uprights did cast shadows, although the shortest shadows of the year. So he went to an obelisk and measured the angle between a line drawn from the tip of the shadow to the tip of the obelisk and the obelisk itself. He found that at the top the angle was seven degrees fourteen minutes.

He then calculated the distance between Syene and Alexandria, possibly by hiring a man to walk it, counting his steps (not easy, given the clumsy Greek number system, which was similar to Roman numerals). More likely he talked with local camel drivers and learned that camels could travel one hundred stadia a day and needed fifty days to get from Syene to Alexandria. The distance between the two cities would thus be five thousand stadia, a common unit of distance, roughly equal to a tenth of a mile. Since seven degrees fourteen minutes is almost exactly one-fiftieth of a circle, it was a simple matter of multiplying five thousand by fifty to determine for the first time the circumference of the earth.

Assuming he used the Egyptian stadia (there were several others in use at the time) his error was roughly 1 percent, an astonishingly precise result given the uncertainties involved. For this and many other accomplishments, Eratosthenes is often called "the father of geography."*

IN THE EARLIEST times, Egyptians built of easily worked local materials, such as wood, reeds, and mud. Then about 2700 B.C., they began building in stone, a material with which Egypt abounds.† But stone is a difficult material to construct with. For one thing, it is heavy. The granite used for obelisks has a specific gravity of about 2.6 (water, by definition, has a specific gravity of 1, so granite weighs 2.6 times as much as the same volume of water). It weighs about 2.1 tons per cubic yard.

And granite is hard, with a hardness index of about 6.5 on the Mohs scale (talc is 1, diamond is 10 on that scale). To

---

* Ironically, about a century later, a Greek named Posidonius used Eratosthenes's basic method, measuring the angle above the horizon of the star Canopus at both Rhodes and Alexandria, to calculate the circumference. Unfortunately he considerably underestimated the distance between the island and the city, and came up with a figure about one-third smaller. It was this figure that Ptolemy used in his second century A.D. text on astronomy, the text that dominated the subject for the next 1,400 years. That is why Columbus was sure he was in Asia when, in fact, he was in a new world.

† Mesopotamia, the other great center of early Western civilization, is an alluvial plain from which stone is largely absent. The rulers there had little choice but to build using mud bricks, which is why, unlike in Egypt, so few ancient structures survive in that area.

work stone, you need something even harder than it is, case-hardened steel chisels, for instance, or diamond-edged saw blades. But the Egyptians had no such tools.

The use of metals had begun about 6000 B.C. Gold was probably the first metal discovered because it occurs in pure form as nuggets and flakes and is easily worked. But gold is far too soft and far too rare to be practical for making tools. Copper is much more abundant and is easily smelted. Heat most copper ores, and the pure metal flows to the bottom of the crucible. Its melting point is only a little over 1,000° Celsius, which was easily reached with the technology of the day. But copper, like gold, is soft and while it will take an edge it does not hold it.

Only when the discovery was made that alloying copper with tin or arsenic produces a metal, bronze, that is far harder than either, could the age of metal tools and weapons really begin. Arsenic is often found in copper ores, so bronze was probably first found accidentally. But arsenic bronze is hard to cast and the fumes of the smelted ores are toxic. It was only when tin began to be used to make bronze, in the late third millennium B.C., that the Bronze Age really began. Copper ore, however, is seldom found in the same area as tin ore, so the wide use of bronze had to wait until extensive, long-distance trade routes were established. The tin mines in far-off Cornwall in England supplied much of the tin of the ancient Mediterranean.

There were seven metals known to the ancients: gold, silver, lead, tin, copper, mercury, and iron. Iron is far more abundant than copper or tin; indeed, it makes up fully

4 percent of the mass of the earth's crust. But its melting point is 1,538° Celsius, a temperature that required special techniques, such as bellows, to reach.

And iron is difficult to work. Only when its complex metallurgy was mastered, by about 1200 B.C., did it begin to replace much more expensive bronze as the principal metal in tool and weapon making. Steel, which is iron with a carefully controlled amount of carbon added, was effectively a semi-precious metal until the nineteenth century when British engineer Sir Henry Bessemer discovered how to make it cheaply in large quantities. Only then could its hardness, ductility, and edge-taking ability be utilized on a grand scale.

The Egyptians had bronze tools by the time of King Menes, about 3150 B.C.; and copper and bronze chisels can be used effectively on limestone, which is much softer than granite, about 3.5 on the Mohs scale. (Limestone was the principle stone used to build the pyramids.) But these tools were far too soft to be effective with granite.

Instead, the Egyptians may have used a green-black stone called dolerite. Dolerite, pounded into roughly the size and shape of softballs, can be found at the quarry near Aswan, in the far south of Egypt, where most obelisks were made. But dolerite is not found there naturally. It was quarried in the eastern desert near the Red Sea, more than a hundred miles away, and taken to Aswan.

Dolerite is an igneous rock but one that is even harder than granite and it deforms less under pressure. Pound granite with balls of dolerite and the granite slowly crumbles into dust, albeit with an infinity of human effort. There

Balls made of dolerite may have helped shape obelisks in ancient Egypt.

were likely hundreds of workers cutting out each obelisk, pounding the granite with balls of dolerite, some of which weighed as much as twelve pounds.

To maintain a steady rhythm it is possible that a method still used in Egypt today was employed: a singer with a gift for extemporizing lyrics. "With a good chanter who can extemporize rhyming lines full of highly flavored personalities," Reginald Engelbach, an English archeologist who was inspector of antiquities for Upper Egypt in the 1920s, wrote, "the work the Egyptians can do is little short of marvelous."

Although the ancient Egyptians left many records behind, thanks to the survivability of papyrus paper in a dry climate, none regarding the quarrying of nor motivation behind the building of obelisks is known.*

---

* One of the realities of historiography is that often people of an earlier time simply didn't write down what we would now like to know. For instance, there is no surviving text from ancient Egypt with instructions for embalming human beings, although that was a deeply important part of the Egyptian religion and they were highly expert at it. Doubtless the reason is that embalming was taught by the apprentice system and, because there was a steady stream of bodies to be mummified, there was no need to write things down. The techniques could be demonstrated instead.

Undoubtedly, part of the attraction of obelisks to successive pharaohs was the sheer difficulty of producing and moving them. As the pharaoh Hatshepsut proudly had inscribed on the base of one of her obelisks at the Temple of Karnak, it was made "without seam, without joining together." Any sovereign capable of ordering and producing such a perfect thing so difficult to construct and erect, must have been rich and powerful indeed. A pharaoh's purpose in ordering the creation of obelisks, therefore, was, in the poet Shelley's words, "Look on my works, ye Mighty, and despair!"

Obelisks were being carved as early as the time of the pyramids, during the Old Kingdom. But while they were more or less obelisk shaped, they were made of many stones and that stone was usually limestone. There is a surviving record from the reign of Pepi II (c. 2278-after 2247 B.C.) of a pair of obelisks being shipped from southern Egypt to Heliopolis, but the obelisks do not survive.

The oldest surviving monolithic (that is to say, one piece) obelisk dates to the reign of Pharaoh Senwosret I (reigned 1965-1920 B.C.), during the Middle Kingdom period. It is about sixty-seven feet high and weighs about 120 tons. Set up before the gateway to a temple in

---

However, we do have detailed instructions on how to mummify a bull. The Apis bull, sacred to the bull-god Apis, lived a life of bovine luxury. When he died of natural causes, he was mummified and buried with elaborate ritual, while a search was mounted to find the next Apis bull, which had to have very precise physical characteristics. Because a bull can easily live to the age of 30 or even 40 years, the instructions for embalming one needed to be written down. The instructions were needed so seldom that they couldn't be transmitted to apprentices by example.

The oldest surviving one-piece obelisk, in Heliopolis, Egypt, almost 4,000 years old.

Heliopolis, it is, today, all that remains of that sanctuary. No other obelisks survive until those created in the New Kingdom, some five hundred years later.

But while we have no written records of how obelisks were quarried, in the quarry at Aswan sits an unfinished obelisk that was left in situ when it cracked during quarrying. Ordered by the female pharaoh Hatshepsut (1508–1458 B.C.), the obelisk would have been huge had it been finished and erected. The Lateran obelisk, now in the square opposite the Cathedral of Saint John Lateran in Rome, is the largest Egyptian obelisk now standing, at 105 feet high and weighing about 400 tons. The unfinished obelisk would have been 137 feet tall and would have weighed 1,200 tons.

Hatshepsut, a highly successful pharaoh, is generally regarded as the first great woman to be known to history. She ruled in her own right as a king, not a queen, and was often depicted wearing the false beard that was the mark of a pharaoh. The daughter of Thutmose I, who reigned early in the New Kingdom, she was the chief wife of Thutmose II, her half brother (incest was a common practice in Egyptian royal dynasties in order to maintain pure blood lines). When Thutmose II died, she served as regent for the infant Thutmose III, a son of Thutmose II by a secondary wife, but soon shoved him aside and took the throne in her own right.

She reestablished trade routes that had been interrupted in an earlier period of foreign conquest by the mysterious Hyksos people. This greatly enriched both

Stone bust of Hatshepsut.

Egypt and the royal coffers. This, in turn, allowed Hatshepsut to embark on a large building program, including four obelisks that reached completion, and her splendid tomb, the first royal tomb built in the Valley of the Kings.*

GARRETT G. FAGAN, professor of ancient history at Pennsylvania State University, wrote that studying ancient history is like trying to study a room by looking through the keyhole.

---

* Of her four obelisks, only one survives upright, at the Temple of Karnak.

Obelisk dedicated to Hatshepsut.

Some parts of the room are perfectly clear and can be described exactly. Others can be half seen and their entirety shrewdly guessed at. But most of the room is invisible.

Our information regarding the construction of an obelisk in ancient Egypt comes almost entirely from the one in-situ obelisk. Thus we don't know many things we would like to know, such as how many men worked on a project, and how long it took to complete. How did they decide what particular part of the quarry they should use? Barring the fortuitous finding of a papyrus detailing construction techniques or a wall painting depicting them, we never will know.

When the trenches along the sides of the aborning obelisk were deep enough the most difficult part of freeing the obelisk, lying flat, from its surrounding rock, undercutting it, began. Again, dolerite balls were likely used until there was only a thin strip of granite still attaching the obelisk to the underlying rock. This, of course, was not only the most difficult part of the process, but also the most dangerous. Misjudge the width of that ever-narrower ledge holding up the obelisk, and it could snap free on its own, crushing the workers in the trenches. Stones were wedged under the shaft of the obelisk to make this less likely.

When the ledge was thin enough, large wooden wedges and, as always, enormous human effort were used to break the obelisk free of the rock. While the obelisk was still being quarried, its polishing and inscribing could begin. Dolerite balls were, again, probably used to smooth and polish the granite while the hieroglyphic inscriptions were carved, perhaps using stone tools and abrasives such as emery.

Once the quarrying was completed, the workers had the challenge of moving the obelisk down to the Nile for transport to the site where it was to be erected.

The Egyptians had simple tools for moving heavy objects, such as the lever, the wedge, the inclined plane, and rollers. They did not have such more sophisticated tools as the compound pulley, which was invented in the third century b.c. by the Greek mathematician and inventor Archimedes.

But mostly they had manpower. Draft animals do not seem to have been used (at least they are not depicted being used in tomb paintings), perhaps because human beings are easier to get to work together in close concert. Ancient Egypt had plenty of manpower as it was densely populated with perhaps eight million people during the New Kingdom. The vast Roman Empire at its height held about seventy million. But while the Roman Empire's population was spread over much of the empire's 2.6 million square miles, Egypt's population was highly concentrated in the Nile Valley, an area of only about fifteen thousand square miles. That would mean a population density of about 533 per square mile.*

Exactly how an obelisk was moved from the quarry to the Nile is not known for sure. Undoubtedly a transport ramp of packed earth and small stones was constructed from the quarry down to the river, made as smooth as possible and wetted to reduce friction. Once the obelisk was freed from the rock, it was levered onto a sledge, which might have been on rollers. Long ropes, probably made of palm fibers, were attached to the sledge for the workers to pull. Even with gravity helping on the downhill run to the river, it would have been slow work.

---

* Modern-day Egypt has a population of about 86 million, by far the largest in the Arab Middle East. But that population still lives in those same 15,000 square miles, the rest of Egypt's 387,000 square miles being almost entirely empty. That makes Egypt effectively the most densely populated country in the world, at about 5,700 people per square mile. That's half again as densely populated as the city of Houston, Texas, the fourth largest in the United States. The Netherlands, the most densely populated country in Europe, has a population density of a little more than 1,000 people per square mile.

Low-relief carvings cut into temple and tomb walls show a colossal human figure being moved on a sledge pulled by hundreds of men. Standing on the statue are one man giving the beat for the concerted pulls and another pouring oil in front of the runners of the sledge to further reduce friction. It has been calculated that two men were needed for a ton of stone to be moved this way. This means the Lateran obelisk would have needed eight hundred men just for hauling—a fraction of the total workforce needed.

A document that survives from the reign of Rameses IV from around 1150 B.C. lists the men needed to haul a monumental stone, perhaps an obelisk, perhaps not, although the size of the stone is not given. In all, 8,162 men were involved: a director of the project, nine high-ranking civil and military officials as well as 362 subordinate ones, artists, stonecutters, 5,000 workmen, and 2,000 armed men, and 800 "men from Ayan" to keep the workmen in order. To give an idea of how dangerous this work was, 900 workmen, more than 10 percent, died in the course of the project.

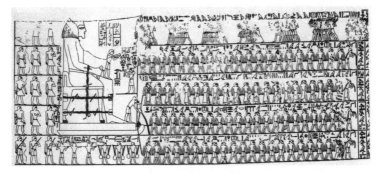

Ancient Egyptian drawing showing the enormous effort needed to move a colossal statue, similar to that required to move an obelisk.

Once the obelisk was at the water's edge, it had to be transferred to a barge and probably the rise and fall of the Nile were utilized in doing so. While the exact nature of this process is unknown, it was surely accomplished only with herculean human effort.

But thanks to a relief carved into the wall of Hatshepsut's funerary temple, we know what happened next. The relief shows two obelisks on the barge, placed end to end. The barge is being towed by three lines of boats with rowers, nine boats in each row and a pilot boat to guide them. Alongside the barge are three boats on which religious ceremonies are being performed. It must have been a considerable spectacle viewed from the shore. Because Aswan is far up the Nile from where the obelisks would be erected, the current helped mightily to move them along.

Finally the challenge of erecting the obelisk on its base, which was usually carved from the same granite as the obelisk itself, was certainly the trickiest and probably most

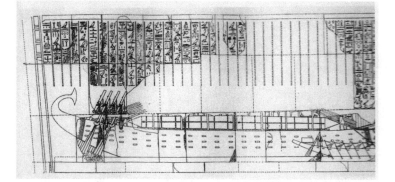

Ancient Egyptian drawing showing two obelisks on a barge, end to end.

dangerous part of the whole process. Again we do not have contemporary evidence of how Egyptians did it. But modern experiments suggest that they might have been erected using the lost-sand method.

In this method, the base is placed in position and then a mud brick wall is built around it, with holes at the bottom. This is filled with sand to the height of the ramp that is used to haul the obelisk into position. When the obelisk is positioned with the center of mass just beyond the edge of the ramp and the base resting on the sand, the holes at the bottom are opened. As the sand pours out, the obelisk slowly descends and, if done right, it lands on the base, its edge in a groove carved into the base. Then ropes are used to haul the obelisk fully upright.* The mud brick walls and the ramp are then demolished and the obelisk is in place for the ages.

There was, of course, only one chance to get it right. The Roman writer Pliny the Elder (A.D. 23–79) recorded that when an obelisk of the pharaoh Rameses, a very large one, was about to be erected, the pharaoh grew nervous. To emphasize the need for care, he "tied his son to the pinnacle, intending that the stone should share the benefit of his deliverance at the hands of the laborers." As Pliny was writing well over a millennium after the event, there is

---

*There is an episode in the PBS *Nova* series that deals with moving and erecting obelisks, including one 25 feet high. The lost-sand method was the successful approach, other methods having failed. There is also a scene early in Cecil B. DeMille's epic movie *The Ten Commandments* that shows Charlton Heston supervising the erection of an obelisk.

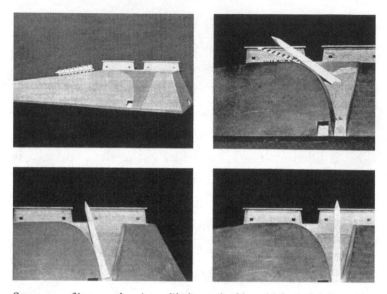

Sequence of images showing a likely method by which obelisks were erected in ancient Egypt.

cause to doubt this tale, which seems a bit too good to be true. But it shows how precarious the operation was and the fact that, if the job was botched, the wrath of the pharaoh was likely to be great.*

---

* Pliny does not say which Rameses he is referring to. But if it was Rameses II, known as Rameses the Great, who reigned from 1279 to 1213 B.C., he had sons to spare. He is known to have fathered more than a hundred.

CHAPTER THREE

Building a Stump

AS ALWAYS WITH the Washington National Monument Society, money was in short supply. As the monument slowly rose after the laying of the cornerstone, various means to increase contributions were attempted. On July 4, 1850, two years after the cornerstone ceremony, a celebration and fund-raising event was held at the monument, attended by the president, Zachary Taylor.

It was a particularly hot day, even by the standards of Washington, D.C., in July. After the event, Taylor returned to the White House and enjoyed cherries and ice-cold milk. He soon fell ill and was diagnosed with cholera morbus, a vague nineteenth-century term for upset stomach, unconnected with Asiatic cholera, which at the time was a frequent cause of deadly epidemics.

The doctors undoubtedly made matters worse, dosing him with ipecac, opium, and even quinine, as well as bleeding him. By July 8 the president was gravely ill and he died the following evening, the second incumbent president to die within a decade. There were persistent reports that he had been poisoned, not an uncommon rumor when very prominent people suddenly sicken and die.

In 1991, his body was exhumed and tested for arsenic, a tasteless poison that produces symptoms not unlike Taylor's. But arsenic levels in his hair, fingernails, and other tissues were not above normal levels. It is altogether likely that his food had been contaminated, as Washington still lacked modern sewers.

WITH THE FOUNDATIONS of the Washington Monument in place and the visible part of the monument about to rise, the state of Alabama in 1850 sent, unsolicited, a block of Alabama marble inscribed with the words, "A Union of Equality, as Adjusted by the Constitution," to be placed in the monument's interior wall. There it could be seen by visitors climbing the stairs to the top.

The society seized on the idea and issued invitations for other states to donate blocks of local stone and instructed that they should be four feet by two feet with a depth of twelve to eighteen inches. The stones were to have the state's name and, if desired, the state coat of arms. States began donating but many paid no attention to the specified dimensions and, often, the specified wording. Today the stones represent a subtle window into the national politics of the 1850s.

It is hard for Americans today to comprehend how fragile the American union was before the Civil War. In those days, the very phrase "the United States" was construed in the plural, "The United States are," as it still is in many foreign languages, such as French. Threats of secession were common.* Many Americans, such as Robert E. Lee, felt that their primary loyalty lay with their state, not the union. As the issue of slavery came to dominate American national politics and the South felt its way of life more and more threatened by a rapidly growing and industrializing North, the union was fraying. This can be clearly seen in the stones placed on the inner walls of the monument.

Illinois's stone reads, "ILLINOIS. State Sovereignty: National Union." Indiana's says, "INDIANA: Knows No North or South, Nothing but the Union." Iowa's says, "IOWA: Her affections, like the rivers of her borders, flow to an inseparable union."

The border state of Missouri's stone reads, "The tribute of Missouri to the memory of Washington and a pledge of her fidelity to the Union of the states." Another border state, Kentucky, pledged that it would be "the Last to Give Up the Union." Even Louisiana, which would be

---

* And not always by southern states. During the War of 1812—wildly unpopular in New England, whose commerce was severely disrupted by it—there were calls for New England to secede and make a separate peace with Great Britain.

Illinois state stone affixed inside the Washington Monument.

the sixth state to secede, on January 26, 1861, sent a stone that read, "The state of Louisiana. Ever faithful to the Constitution and the Union." Tennessee, which would be the last state to secede and join the Confederacy, sent a stone that read, "TENNESSEE: FEDERAL UNION It must be preserved."*

Not only states sent stones to be installed in the monument; cities did as well as twenty-two Masonic lodges, twelve Odd Fellows lodges, and seven fire departments. Eight Sons of Temperance lodges also sent stones, the one from Pennsylvania proclaiming that "The surest Safeguard of the liberty of our country is total abstinence from all that

---

*The Tennessee stone was not actually installed until 1880, at the 230-foot level. It had a rather checkered history. Received in 1851, it had not yet been installed in 1855 when it was mutilated by having three slabs removed from the back and used for table tops. The city of Nashville's stone had been put in place in 1850.

intoxicates." A few individuals contributed stones, but the society stopped accepting personal stones in 1849.

Foreign countries also began sending stones, including Wales (the inscription, in Welsh, reads, "Our Language, our country, our birthplace. Wales forever"). Siam (now Thailand), Turkey, Greece, China, Japan, and the Swiss Confederation sent stones. Commodore Matthew Perry, on his way back from negotiating the opening of Japan in 1854, stopped at Okinawa where he received a stone in honor of "the great Mandarin," George Washington. The stone mysteriously disappeared during the Civil War and was not replaced until 1989.

In all, 195 stones now adorn the inner walls of the Washington Monument.*

By far the most famous of the Washington Monument commemorative stones is the one that isn't there, the stone donated by the Vatican early in 1854.

Made of stone that had originally been part of the Temple of Concord in the Roman Forum, it measured three feet wide and eighteen inches high and had a depth of ten inches.† On the night of March 5, 1854, a group of men

---

* In the 1970s, to prevent vandals from chipping chunks off the stones, the National Park Service closed the stairs and today one can only reach the top of the monument via the elevator. There are plans to put windows in the elevator and light the stones so that they can be, once again, seen.

† The Temple of Concord, although rebuilt several times, dated back to 367 B.C. when it was vowed by Marcus Furius Camillus (c.445 B.C.-365 B.C.) after he engineered a compromise in the long dispute between the Plebeians and Patricians. A major figure in early Roman history, Camillus was later dubbed by Plutarch "the second founder of Rome." The temple was finally destroyed about A.D. 1450, when its stones were quarried for other uses.

broke into the monument's construction site, tied a clothes-line around the watchman's watch box, piled stones against the door, and pasted newspapers across the windows. He was told that if he kept quiet, he would not be harmed and, although he could easily have broken out—he had a double-barreled shotgun with him—he made no attempt to do so. He was promptly fired for failing to do his job.

The intruders took the "Pope's stone," as it was usually called, and carted it off to the Potomac River, where they either broke it into pieces or defaced it and threw it into the river. Its fate has never been determined for sure, although numerous rumors swirled around it.*

On March 8, the *Daily National Intelligencer* was outraged by this wanton act of vandalism. "A deed of barbarism," it wrote, "was enacted on Monday morning last, between one and two o'clock, by several persons . . . which will be considered as belonging rather to some of the centuries considerably in our rear than to the better half of the boasted Nineteenth Century. We refer to the forcible seizure from its place of deposit, in a shed at the Washington Monument, of a block of marble sent hither from Rome, a tribute to the memory of Washington by the Pontiff, and intended to become a part of the edifice now erecting to signalize his name and glory."

Also on March 8, the society placed an advertisement in the *Intelligencer*:

---

* The Pope's stone was eventually replaced, but not until 1982, when a new one made of Carerra marble was sent, bearing the same inscription the original had had, "A Roma Americae", "From Rome to America."

$100 REWARD.
The Board of Managers of the
Washington National Monument Society
will pay the above reward of $100 for the arrest and
conviction of the person or persons who,
on the night of the 5th instant,
stole and destroyed a block of marble
contributed to said Monument.

Not surprisingly, no one was ever arrested for this crime, but everyone was sure who had done it: the Know-Nothings.

In the 1850s the United States was rapidly changing demographically. In the first half of that decade immigration was five times higher than it had been a decade earlier and the new immigrants did not fit in easily among the overwhelmingly Protestant, native-born population. The Irish potato famine and political unrest in the German states caused a surge of Catholic immigrants, most of them the poorest of the poor, in many cases illiterate and unskilled. They squeezed into rapidly growing slums, such as the notorious Five Points section of lower Manhattan, which was soon among the most densely populated urban neighborhoods on earth.

Charles Dickens visited Five Points on his first trip to America in 1842. "What place is this," he wrote in his *American Notes*, "to which the squalid street conducts us? A kind of square of leprous houses, some of which are attainable only by crazy wooden stairs without. What lies behind this tottering flight of steps? Let us go on again, and plunge into the Five Points . . . This is the place: these narrow ways diverging to the right and left, and reeking everywhere with dirt and filth."

With American cities filling up with poor immigrants, many of whom did not speak English, there was a surge in crime and violence. In Cincinnati, between 1846 and 1853, crime rose 300 percent, while the murder rate went up by a factor of seven in those years. Other American cities had similar increases in crime.

Naturally this provoked an intense backlash against both immigrants in general and Catholics in particular. When Pope Pius IX sent his stone, there was much opposition to having it installed. Newspaper editorials against the stone were common, as were petitions sent to the society. One from New Jersey raged that

> the proffer of a block of marble recently made by the pope of Rome to this country for the Washington Monument [is] totally inconsistent with the known principles of that despotic system of government of which he is the head; . . . that the construction is an artful stratagem, calculated to divert attention of the American people for the present from his animosity to republican institutions by an outward profession of regard; that the gift of a despot, if placed within those walls, can never be looked upon by true Americans but with feelings of mortification and disgust . . .

Across the country in the 1840s and early 1850s, semi-secret groups began to coalesce into a political party, often called the Native American Party or just the American Party. But because members of these groups were instructed to say, when asked about the group, "I know nothing," they became known as the Know-Nothings.

As the Whig Party collapsed in the early 1850s, the Know-Nothings picked up more support and had some political success. In the election of 1854 they sent no fewer than fifty-two men to Congress, including Nathaniel P. Banks of Massachusetts, who, after a long and bitter fight (and 133 ballots), was elected speaker of the House of Representatives. But Banks, and other antislavery Know-Nothings, soon joined the new Republican Party, founded in 1854. The Know-Nothings faded away as American politics, increasingly torn apart by the issue of slavery, coalesced around the Democratic and the Republican parties that have dominated the nation's politics ever since.

THE VANDALISM OF the pope's stone only complicated the society's effort to raise funds. Catholics, deeply offended, stopped giving, and a slowdown in the American economy also caused contributions to dry up. By 1854, the monument had risen to the height of 153 feet and the society had expended two hundred thirty thousand dollars.

Once again, it petitioned Congress for action and the House established a select committee to look into the

Certificate given to anyone contributing to the building of the
Washington Monument.

matter, under the chairmanship of freshman congressman
Henry May of Baltimore.*

Representative May reported to the House on
February 22, 1855, praising the society for its scrupulous care
of the funds that had been donated and recommended that

---

* May, who had been elected as a Democrat, served only one term before being
defeated for reelection in 1856; he was elected again as a Unionist in 1860. In
September 1861, Abraham Lincoln, who had suspended habeas corpus on his own
authority, had May arrested on suspicion of treason and held in Fort Lafayette.

The Constitution allows the suspension of habeas corpus in times of emergency, but
the language is in Article I, which establishes and grants powers to Congress, not Article
II, which establishes the executive and grants powers to the president. So Lincoln was
pushing his authority very far. Indeed, Chief Justice Roger Taney, sitting as a circuit
court judge, ruled Lincoln's action unconstitutional, a ruling that Lincoln ignored.

No charges were ever brought against May and he was released in December and
returned to Congress. There he introduced a bill to require that "political prisoners" be
either indicted by grand jury or released. His language was incorporated in the Habeas
Corpus Act of 1863, which, belatedly, empowered Lincoln to suspend the civil right.

Congress appropriate two hundred thousand dollars "on behalf of the people of the United States to *aid* the funds of this Society." This was not to be a Congressional takeover, simply a contribution to the society.

It appeared likely that Congress, which had first appropriated two hundred thousand dollars way back in 1801 to build a mausoleum for Washington in the District of Columbia, would finally help the society financially.

But as May was speaking before the House, he was handed a note and immediately asked that the matter be suspended. The reason was that the night before, the Washington National Monument Society had been taken over by what might be called a *coup de société*: The Know-Nothings had seized control of the Washington Monument.

On February 21, 1855, notices had appeared in newspapers, signed by F. W. Eckloff, the clerk of the society, announcing an election for the board of the society. It was completely at odds with the constitution of the organization, which called for the next election to be held the following year, and Eckloff had no authority to call for an election, which was the duty of the secretary.

On February 22, 755 people showed up in response to the notice, and voted unanimously for seventeen men as officers and board members of the society, none of them members of the existing board. The voters held certificates of membership, which could be had for the price of a dollar, but no money for these certificates was received by the society's treasurer.

The regular board promptly declared "that the election held on the 22d instant of officers and managers of the Washington National Monument Society was in direct violation of the Constitution of the Society, and therefore null and void." It proposed that "an amicable suit be instituted for the purpose of testing the rights of the two parties."

The two boards met on March 3, but could not agree on anything. The Know-Nothing board flatly refused to submit the dispute to the courts, doubtless knowing that it would lose if it did.

The superintendent of the project refused to turn over possession of the building site to the new board and so on March 9, the Know-Nothings seized it forcibly and appointed a new superintendent.

In May, the new board put out a manifesto, addressed to the "Brethren of the American Party," giving its reasons for the coup. Principal among them was the pope's stone.

"It was an American Monument," the document read, "and its construction and management was said to be mainly in the hands of Catholics and foreigners. . . . For these and diverse other causes, the Americans of this District resolved in their respective Councils that this work ought to be typical of their government, completed by the free act of the People, under the direction and by the hands of the natives."

The Know-Nothing board received little if any money in the way of contributions. Neither did the regular board, which reported that while it had received $695 in contributions between January 3 and February 20, it received only $51.66 during the remainder of the year.

The Know-Nothings tried to continue with construction and added two courses of stone during the next two years. But they had no choice but to use the stone on hand, all of which had been rejected by the previous superintendent as unfit for use.

By the late 1850s the American Party was rapidly collapsing and on October 20, 1858, the Know-Nothing board surrendered the books, papers, office, and the monument itself to the regular board. It also turned over $285.09. How much more it had collected in the previous three years is unknown.

At a meeting on December 28, 1858, the restored board reported that the engine house and other buildings on the site were in dilapidated condition, although the engine and boiler were sound. Also of two large cranes used to lift stone from the wharves, one had fallen down and one had disappeared. The report estimated that "it will require an expenditure of at least $2000 to place the fixtures and machinery in a condition to enable your Board to resume the progress of the work."

BECAUSE THE SOCIETY had been a voluntary association, it had been hamstrung in its legal attempts to recover its property from the Know-Nothings. Therefore it now asked Congress to establish it by charter and this was granted on February 22, 1859. President James Buchanan signed it into law on the 26th. The charter gave the society the right to sue and be sued, and made the members of the society liable in their personal capacity for any indebtedness of the society itself.

A month later, the society was officially reorganized under the terms of the new charter. President Buchanan, as the ex officio president of the society, presided over the meeting. He recalled that as a member of Congress in 1824 he had tried to interest the House in erecting a monument to Washington, but "it was considered at that time, and so remarked in Congress, that it was rather an indignity that any effort should be made to raise a monument to the honor and memory of Washington besides that which existed in the hearts of his countrymen."

New officers were elected, including Lieutenant General Winfield Scott, commanding general of the Army and one of the great generals in American history. A new plan for raising money was adopted, and contribution boxes were put out at polling places on election days. But at the election in Washington on June 6, 1859, a mere $150.76 was collected. A local newspaper attributed the poor showing to the fact that the monument had been in the hands of a political faction for three years and little had been accomplished. It noted that

> It was not till this state of things unhappily took place
> that the popular enthusiasm drooped and cooled, and it
> is hardly fair to expect a resurrection in an hour or a day.
> We trust, however, that the night is far spent; that the

day is at hand, and even the tribute of the voters of Washington on Monday last, small as it was, is an evidence of new life and returning vigor."

That vigor was hard to discern. For all of 1859, the society took in just $3,074.96. It had spent $1,429.39 that year. The society had estimated that it would require about forty-five thousand dollars a year in contributions to keep construction of the monument progressing steadily.

THAT YEAR THE society asked the secretary of the Army to appoint an officer of the topographical engineering corps to serve as engineer of the monument and supervise its construction. The secretary appointed Lieutenant J. C. Ives to the post.

Joseph Christmas Ives (his middle name came from the fact that he was born on Christmas day, 1829) graduated from West Point in 1852 and was soon appointed to the topographical engineering corps. In 1857–58, he commanded an expedition up the Colorado River. He designed and built a fifty-four-foot stern-wheel steamboat, disassembled it, and shipped it to the mouth of the Colorado River where he reassembled it.* The expedition steamed, with difficulty, as far as the rapids at Black Canyon, close to where Las Vegas stands today and the

---

* The Colorado River today is so heavily dammed and its water so heavily used for irrigation that it no longer reaches the sea. So Ives's expedition would be impossible today.

lower entrance to the Grand Canyon. There they struck a rock and the ship was abandoned. They proceeded to explore the Grand Canyon before heading home.

Ives was not impressed with what he found. He wrote in his journal,

> It [the Grand Canyon] looks like the Gates of Hell. The region . . . is, of course, altogether valueless. Ours has been the first and will undoubtedly be the last, party of whites to visit the locality. It seems intended by nature that the Colorado River along the greater portion of its lonely and majestic way, shall be forever unvisited and undisturbed.

Ives was as mistaken as to his priority as he was in his prediction. The Grand Canyon had first been seen by a Spanish expedition led by García López de Cárdenas in 1540. Ives and his men may not have even been the first Americans, other than local Indians of course, to see what is today regarded as one of the country's greatest natural wonders. But his was the first official expedition and it produced an important map that would later be used by John Wesley Powell's far more consequential expedition in 1869.

Although northern by birth, Ives had married into the Semmes family of Maryland. His wife's cousin was Captain Raphael Semmes who commanded the Confederate commerce raider CSS *Alabama*. On the outbreak of the war, in April 1861, Ives resigned from the U.S. Army and joined the Confederate Army, rising to the rank of colonel. In 1863 he was appointed an aide-de-camp to President Jefferson Davis.

While still supervisor of the Washington Monument, before the outbreak of the war, Ives was asked to report on both the stability of the materials being used in construction and the adequacy of the foundation to support the weight of the completed monument. He reported that the foundations were now bearing about four sevenths of the final weight and that he had been unable to detect any shifting. He also calculated that the completed monument would be able to withstand, by a factor of eight, any storm likely to be encountered.

Ives also proposed a new fund-raising scheme, suggesting putting out donation boxes in every post office in the country and putting postmasters in charge of monitoring the boxes and transmitting the money to Washington.

The results were disappointing, as the society's fund-raising efforts usually were. Four months into the project, the society had received $2,240.31 from 841 post offices and nothing from more than 28,000. Ives lamented that the postmaster general had not cooperated. He was sure that if he had, most if not all of the nation's post offices would have taken part in the plan.

A Ladies' Association was formed in 1859 to also help with the fund-raising, but, again, with very disappointing results. In 1860 it raised only $458.50.

On March 26, 1861, three weeks after Abraham Lincoln had been inaugurated and when seven states had already seceded from the Union, the society appealed once more.

"In consequence of the great falling off in post-office contributions, ascribable chiefly to the troubles of the times and the usual change on the advent of a new administration, the undersigned deem it proper to again appeal to the patriotism of the people and postmasters." But in all of 1861, the post-office contributions amounted to only $88.52. Rhode Island contributed seventy-five cents, Virginia forty-eight cents, and Mississippi fifteen cents. Congress, as well, refused to make an appropriation. With the nation

The Washington Monument circa 1860, at the start of the Civil War.

on the brink of civil war, people had other things to worry about than a truncated obelisk 170 feet high.*

As volunteers poured into Washington after the firing on Fort Sumter in April 1861, they at first bivouacked on the grounds surrounding the monument. It later became a drilling field and then a pasture for the cattle driven into the city to feed the troops.

On Washington's birthday in 1862, a Navy Yard rigger made it to the top of the monument and raised the stars and stripes. It was a sad gesture. As one modern-day historian, Thomas B. Allen, explained, "The flag symbolized the Union, but it flew over an ugly stump that symbolized a sundered nation."

---

* Lincoln understood the power of symbolism. While the unfinished monument languished, he insisted that the construction of the Capitol dome, authorized in 1855, be continued as a promise that the union would survive. Made of cast iron, the pieces of the dome were fabricated in the Bronx and shipped by railroad to Washington, where the pieces were bolted together, not unlike an Erector set. In December 1863, the Statue of Freedom was placed atop the dome.

CHAPTER FOUR

Stealing Obelisks

FEWER THAN A quarter of the surviving Egyptian obelisks are in Egypt. The rest are mostly in cities scattered around the Mediterranean littoral. Three more are in London, Paris, and New York and a few more smaller ones stand elsewhere.* There are no fewer than eleven in the city of Rome alone, plus four more that the Romans made.

---

* The most famous of these smaller obelisks is the so-called Philae obelisk, after the place in Egypt where it was found. It is about twenty-one feet tall and weighs six tons. It was discovered by William John Bankes, one of the great Egyptologists and antiquarians of his day, in 1815. He had it transported to his family estate, Kingston Lacy, in Dorset, England, where it stands today in the gardens. Its dedication ceremony at Kingston Lacy was presided over by the Duke of Wellington, whom Bankes had served as an aide-de-camp in the Peninsular War. The Philae obelisk would turn out to be a vital clue to deciphering hieroglyphics.

Most of these scattered obelisks are where they are as trophies, taken without so much as a by-your-leave by foreigners who ruled over—or had great influence over—Egypt in the post-Pharaonic era.

The first of these trophy hunters was Caesar Augustus, the first emperor of Rome.

The Roman Republic that had been established in 509 B.C., after the expulsion of Rome's kings, died in the agony of civil war. A long series of these wars stretched over a hundred years, beginning in the late second century B.C. The wars finally ended, in 30 B.C. in, of all places, Egypt.

With the assassination of Julius Caesar in 44 B.C., Caesar's adopted son, Octavian, and Mark Antony sought vengeance on the assassins, forming the so-called Second Triumvirate with Marcus Lepidus. With the assassins vanquished and Lepidus squeezed out, Octavian and Antony divided the Roman world between them, Antony taking the east—where he soon fell in love with Cleopatra—and Octavian the west.

This was, not surprisingly, an unstable arrangement, especially given the fact that while Antony was married to Octavian's sister, he was living with and having children by Cleopatra.

Soon at war with each other, the two antagonists met at Actium in western Greece, where Antony's forces were

---

Bankes, an inveterate traveler and adventurer, assembled the largest collection of Egyptian antiquities of the early nineteenth century, much of which can be seen today at Kingston Lacy, now part of the National Trust. He was elected a Fellow of the Royal Society in 1822.

decisively defeated in a naval battle in 31 B.C. and he and Cleopatra fled to Egypt. Octavian followed them there and, in 30 B.C., both Antony and Cleopatra committed suicide, Antony by falling on his sword and Cleopatra supposedly by the bite of an asp, a venomous snake, possibly a cobra.

Egypt was declared a province of Rome, and Egyptian sources list Octavian as the next pharaoh. Octavian, who soon took the name Augustus, treated Egypt as his private preserve and senators were not allowed to go there without Augustus's personal permission.

But while Octavian treated it as nearly his personal property it was quickly integrated economically into the

Caesar Augustus.

empire. The great granary of the ancient Mediterranean world, Egypt was soon shipping upward of five million bushels of grain to Rome every year, about one third of the city's total grain supply. In 27 B.C., Augustus became the first emperor of Rome.*

He also soon began moving, and removing, obelisks in and from his new province. A pair that had stood at Heliopolis was moved on his orders to Alexandria to ornament the Caesareum, a temple, originally built by Cleopatra and meant as a mausoleum for Mark Antony. Augustus dedicated it to Julius Caesar, who had been declared divine.† In 10 B.C. he began moving obelisks all the way to Rome.

The Egyptians had necessarily mastered the art of moving obelisks by water. But the smooth, gentle waters of the Nile are one thing, the often treacherous waters of the Mediterranean quite another. Storms can blow up quickly in the sea that the Romans by this time had taken to calling Mare Nostrum ("Our Sea"). So it was the custom to stick close to the shore as much as possible and to venture

---

* While the English word *emperor* derives from the Latin *imperator*, the two words have very different meanings. In ancient Rome, *imperator* simply meant someone who possessed *imperium*, the power to act in the name of the state, as a governor appointed by the Senate would have in a given province. Augustus's imperium effectively reached throughout the empire, but there was no sense of royalty or sovereignty attached to the title. Rome had had an intense antimonarchical bent in its politics since the kings had been expelled. During the days of the republic, accusing a powerful politician of wanting to become king was a common way of attacking him. Sovereignty, at least in theory, remained with the "Senatus Populusque Romanus," the Senate and People of Rome, SPQR for short. Augustus preferred the title Princeps Civitatis, "First Citizen." Only in the fourth century, in the time of the Emperor Constantine, did Roman emperors begin to take on royal trappings.
† They are now the obelisks in London and New York.

across open waters only at the Mediterranean's narrowest points.

No ordinary ships from ancient times survive, for while we have discovered many shipwrecks, the ships, constructed of wood, have always long since rotted away, leaving only their cargoes. By far the best-preserved ship of early civilization dates back, remarkably, to the time of the pyramids. In 1954 the unassembled pieces of a ship, perfectly preserved, were found next to the great pyramid of Khufu at Giza. It took years to reassemble and proved to be more than 140 feet long and powered by oars.* But this vessel was clearly a ceremonial ship, meant for Nile waters if it was meant for actual use at all.

Seagoing cargo ships in everyday commerce would have been far more robustly constructed, probably with both a sail and oars, using a stern oar to keep course. They would have been relatively deep drafted to maximize cargo capacity, which could amount to hundreds of tons.

These ships were capable of considerable feats of navigation. According to Herodotus, a fleet of Phoenician ships, at the behest of Pharaoh Necho II (ruled 610–595 B.C.), circumnavigated Africa, starting out from a Red Sea port, and taking three years to make the trip. (They would stop in the spring, plant grain, and wait for the harvest before setting out again.) Many, in both ancient and modern times, have doubted Herodotus's story. But he noted, in some disbelief, that the sailors reported that when

---

* It has been on display at Giza since 1983.

sailing westward below the African landmass, the sun was on their right, i.e., to the north, as indeed it would be in the southern hemisphere.

But an ordinary merchant ship of the time of Jesus, perhaps eighty feet long, could not have dealt with an obelisk. Indeed, successfully transporting an Egyptian obelisk across the Mediterranean was regarded by commentators of the time, such as Pliny the Elder, as a greater wonder than the obelisk itself. As always with obelisks, the sheer difficulty of dealing with them was a symbol and example of the leader's power.

According to Pliny, the Romans used a triple-hulled ship, with the obelisk resting on the middle hull, which was placed forward of the other, outboard, two hulls. It would be taken on board by ballasting the other two hulls until the middle hull was at water level and, once the obelisk had been heaved aboard, removing the ballast. Some sources say that these ships, in addition to their own sail power, were also towed by a trireme, a warship powered by 120 oars.

The ship that carried the first obelisk to Rome was regarded as so extraordinary that it was put on display at a permanent dock before being destroyed by fire a few decades later. Another obelisk ship, used in the time of Caligula (ruled A.D. 37–41), was sunk and filled with concrete and formed part of the harbor works of Ostia, the port of Rome. It was found in the 1950s and, while the ship itself was long gone, the concrete retained a partial impression of the ship.

Once ashore, moving and erecting the obelisk was far less of a problem for the Romans than the Egyptians. The greatest engineers of the ancient world, the Romans had the compound pulley—invented by Archimedes in the third century B.C. A series of single pulleys, it multiplies the force being applied, allowing the lifting of great weights with far less human or animal muscle power. The great mathematician himself is reported to have moved an entire warship, loaded with men, single-handed, thanks to the compound pulley.

In addition, the Romans were masters of siege warfare. Siege engines, used for attacking city walls, were adapted,

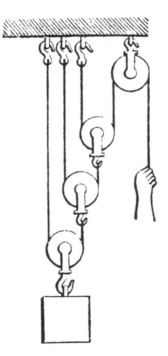

A compound pulley system.

as hoists and cranes, to lift great weights in construction projects, such as the aqueducts that carried water to Roman cities. These hoists were often powered by men in a "squirrel cage," a large rotating drum.

Crucially, the Romans, unlike the Egyptians of a millennium and a half earlier, had iron. Its use, both in implements and in constructing the great cranes and hoists, allowed for the manipulation of prodigious weights.*

The first Egyptian obelisk taken to Rome by Augustus in 10 B.C. stands today in the Piazza di Monte Citorio. It is seventy-one feet high and weighs about two hundred tons, and was carved on orders of Pharaoh Psammetichus II (ruled c. 593–c. 588 B.C.), who had inscribed on it his relationship to Ra, the Egyptian sun god. As Egyptian pharaohs had often added inscriptions to obelisks erected by their predecessors, Augustus did also. Translated into English, the heavily abbreviated Latin reads

---

* Much of what we know about Roman construction techniques, and the machinery used in construction, comes to us thanks to a Roman architect remembered as Vitruvius, who lived in the first century B.C. His book *De Architectura*, dedicated to Augustus, miraculously survives complete, except for the illustrations, the only ancient text on architecture to do so. It deeply influenced the architecture of the Renaissance. Brunelleschi used it in designing a hoist to help build the dome of the Cathedral in Florence in the fifteenth century.

De Architectura is also the ultimate source of the famous story about Archimedes getting into a bath and, noticing the water level rising, suddenly understanding the principle of displacement, which allowed the determination of the volume of irregular objects. He was so excited that, at least according to the story—and this would have caused far less comment in ancient Syracuse than it would today— he ran down the streets of Syracuse stark naked yelling "Eureka!" Greek for "I have found it!"

Caesar, emperor, son of the deified Julius, Augustus, chief priest, imperator for the twelfth time, consul for the eleventh, holder of tribunician power for the fourteenth time, Egypt having been brought under the rule of the Roman people, he gave this as a gift to Sol [a Roman personification of the sun].

It was originally erected in the area of Rome known as the Campus Martius, where it served as the gnomon of a huge sundial. Pliny the Elder wrote that it

marked the shadows projected by the sun, and so measuring the length of the days and nights. With this object, a stone monument was laid, the extreme length of which corresponded exactly with the length of the shadow thrown by the obelisk at the sixth hour [i.e., noon] on the day of the winter solstice. After this period the shadow would go on day by day, gradually decreasing, and then again would as gradually increase, correspondingly with certain lines of brass that were inserted in the stone.

If this description is accurate, then the whole functioned not only as a clock, telling the time of day, but as a calendar, telling the time of the year. Pliny, writing in the seventies A.D., noted that it had not been accurate for about thirty years, perhaps due to settling of the massive stone, despite a foundation that Pliny reported to be as deep as the obelisk was high. It is equally possible that a minor earthquake, which are far more common in Italy than in Egypt, might have caused it to tilt.

The obelisk remained standing until sometime in the tenth or eleventh century, when it fell and broke into five pieces, perhaps due to fire or earthquake. Soon buried by sediment, it was only rediscovered in the reign of Pope Julius II (reigned 1503–13), by a barber digging a latrine.* Pope Sixtus V (reigned 1585–90), who had a great interest in obelisks, wanted to reerect it and even ordered a bronze globe with holes in it for its top, so that it could once again function as a sundial. But its condition was so poor that it was soon reburied.

Pope Alexander VII (1655–67) also tried but failed to restore the obelisk. Pope Benedict XIV (1740–58) had it removed from the square where it had lain, then surrounded by derelict buildings but now the site of the Italian Parliament building.

Finally, in the reign of Pius VI (1775–99), the obelisk was restored. To repair it, red granite from the toppled column of the emperor Antoninus Pius (reigned 138–161) was used.† After three years it was finally erected in its present location and Pius VI added his own inscription.

---

* Rome had a population of about a million at the height of the empire. But by the Middle Ages the population had fallen perhaps as low as 30,000, a mere 3 percent of its ancient population. So there were vast areas of the earlier city that had been abandoned, and many of its ancient buildings were used as quarries for building new buildings.

† The base of the column is now in the Vatican Museums. It shows Antoninus and his wife being carried to heaven. A personification of the Field of Mars holds the obelisk.

The first Egyptian obelisk taken to Rome, now in the Piazza di Monte Citorio.

NO POPE DID more to restore Rome's Egyptian obelisks than Sixtus V, during his short reign from 1585 to 1590. Born into a poor family in the Papal States in 1521, while still very young he entered the Franciscan friary at Montalto, which he adopted as his last name, and soon showed extraordinary talents, both as a preacher and as a philosopher.

By the time he was in his thirties he had come to the attention of the head of the Franciscan order as well as two cardinals who would themselves be later elected pope. With this backing he advanced up the church hierarchy quickly.

He was made inquisitor general of Venice, but took the job so seriously that that morally easygoing city asked for his recall.

In 1565 he was attached to the Spanish legation headed by Ugo Cardinal Boncampagni, sent to Spain to investigate the charges of heresy against the archbishop of Toledo. He and Boncampagni developed a thorough dislike of each other. Returned to Rome, he was made a cardinal by Pope Pius V in 1570.

During the pontificate of Cardinal Boncampagni, who reigned as Gregory XIII from 1572 to 1585, he was in forced retirement.* But upon Gregory's death in 1585, he was elected pope.

Sixtus V restored four of Rome's Egyptian obelisks. The Flaminio obelisk is one of them. It originally stood about seventy-eight feet high and weighed 235 tons; it was taken to Rome in the same year as the one in the Piazza di Monte Citorio and has an identical inscription. Augustus had it placed in the center of the Circus Maximus, the arena where chariot races were held, on the "spina," the thin strip in the center of the racecourse.†

---

* Pope Gregory XIII is best remembered today as the pope who ordered the reform of the Julian calendar to bring it back into conformity with astronomical reality. The Julian calendar is off by eleven minutes a year. After 1500 years it had become ten days behind reality. In 1582, Gregory ordered that October 5 be followed by October 15 (much to the disgruntlement of renters and the pleasure of landlords) and that in the future three leap days be dropped from every 400 years. The Gregorian calendar is so accurate, off by only twenty-six seconds a year, that it won't be a full day off until the year 4909.
† The Circus Maximus was a colossal structure (whence the name, which means "largest circus"). Some 2,037 feet long and 387 feet wide, it could hold 150,000

In his five years as pope, Sixtus V did much to restore Rome's Egyptian obelisks.

The Circus Maximus fell into disuse in the fifth century and it is not known when or how the obelisk fell. It was lost until the fifteenth century and in 1586, Sixtus V had it restored and placed in the Piazza del Popolo. The bottom portion, with an inscription placed on it by Augustus, was removed and was added to the base.

Sixtus V also reerected an obelisk that had been commissioned by the emperor Domitian (A.D. 81–96), one

---

people. The chariot races were one of the major sporting events of ancient Rome and were often lethal to the participants, horses and men alike. The famous chariot race scene in *Ben-Hur* (1959), one of the greatest of Hollywood's cast-of-thousands scenes, is probably the best depiction of what these races were like.

of a pair. Originally placed before the mausoleum of Augustus, it broke in two pieces when it fell and Sixtus had it placed in the Piazza dell'Esquilino behind the Church of Santa Maria Maggiore.

Sixtus's third restoration is known as the Lateran obelisk and it now stands in the square in front of the Cathedral of Saint John Lateran and the Lateran Palace. Originally ordered by Thutmose III, it was transported to Rome by the emperor Constantius (reigned 337–361), the son of Constantine I, Rome's first Christian emperor. He had it erected on the spina of the Circus Maximus, a pair with the Flaminio obelisk. Like its mate, it fell at some

The Lateran obelisk.

point in the Middle Ages and broke into three pieces. Dug up in 1587, the pieces were reassembled, although the obelisk is now thirteen feet shorter than it was in ancient times. But it is still the tallest obelisk in Rome, at 104 feet, and weighs perhaps as much as 425 tons.

By far the most famous obelisk in Rome, however, is in Saint Peter's Square. It, too, was the work of Sixtus V.

Eighty-three feet tall and weighing an estimated 325 tons, it is the only Egyptian obelisk in Rome to lack hieroglyphics, so its earlier history is not clear. But it was certainly moved to Alexandria at the order of Augustus and then, in A.D. 37, the emperor Caligula ordered it moved to Rome.

He placed it on the spina of a new circus, the Circus of Caligula, later remembered as the Circus of Nero, as the emperor Nero (reigned A.D. 54–68) used it for the first Christian martyrdoms.

The Great Fire of Rome broke out on the night of July 18, A.D. 64. Nero, needing a scapegoat, blamed it on the new Christian sect that was becoming established in cities in the empire, and he ordered the first Christian persecution. Among those killed in the slaughter was Saint Peter, the first pope. The obelisk thus was a witness to the martyrdom of Saint Peter and held a special place in the hearts of Christians.

According to legend, Peter, informed that he was to be crucified, said that he was unworthy to die in the same manner as Jesus, so he was crucified upside down. After his gruesome death, he was buried a few hundred yards away from where he had died in the Circus Nero.

The circus was located partially where Saint Peter's Basilica stands today, upon the site where Saint Peter was buried.* Early in the fourth century, the emperor Constantine began building the first Saint Peter's Basilica.† Beside that basilica stood the obelisk that had been erected by Caligula more than 250 years earlier. It continued to stand there for the next 1,100 years, the only Egyptian obelisk in Rome that never toppled.

In 1506, Pope Julius II ordered the construction of a new basilica, the one we are familiar with today. He also suggested moving the obelisk to the front of the new building. His architect, Donato Bramante, suggested instead moving the basilica, orienting it south instead of east. But Julius declined that idea because then the basilica would not be sited over the grave of Saint Peter.

In the middle of the sixteenth century, Pope Paul III tried to get his architect, Michelangelo, to move the obelisk but the great artist would not try it. Asked why, he replied, "And if it were broken?"

In all more than 120 years were needed to complete the building (and the colonnades surrounding Saint Peter's square would not be completed until forty years later still).

---

* After ten years of excavations, in 1950 Pope Pius XII announced that the tomb of Saint Peter had been located. What was found were bones wrapped in a cloth that would have been very expensive in the first century and so were clearly the remains of a man of great importance, located in a place where no pagan Roman of importance would have been buried. So, by inference, it was Saint Peter.

† Saint Peter's is a basilica—a church with special papal privileges, often built on a holy site—not a cathedral. The cathedral of the pope, the bishop of Rome, is Saint John Lateran.

When Sixtus V came to the throne of Saint Peter, the great building was not even half completed and the dome, which today is still the highest in the world, was less than half done.

An energetic pope, Sixtus V accelerated the building process considerably and by the time of his death five years later, the dome was completed, although the lantern on top would not be erected for another few years.

And in the midst of all this construction, Sixtus determined, once and for all, to move Caligula's obelisk and reerect it in the middle of what would become Saint Peter's Square. For that, of course, he would need an engineer of surpassing skill.

Sixtus called on a committee that handled the building and maintenance of Rome's infrastructure to choose one but instead it offered a prize for the best plan to move the obelisk. As would happen later in other obelisk moves, some fairly crackpot ideas were submitted to the committee. One wanted to take it down and then reerect it by means of a huge wheel, another to lower it to a forty-five degree angle and move it in that position. Another wanted to use a variation on Archimedes' screw.

Domenico Fontana submitted the winning plan, which involved lowering the obelisk, moving it the three hundred yards to its new site on rollers, and then reerecting it by means of ropes and capstans. The capstan, a ratcheted drum, turned by poles, was a Spanish invention, used on ships to raise anchors and other heavy weights— technology that had been unavailable to both Egyptians and Romans.

Domenico Fontana, who moved the obelisk to St. Peter's Square in Rome.

Fontana produced a scale model of his proposal, complete with a lead obelisk, to show the committee exactly what he intended to do.

He was already well known to Sixtus, who had entrusted the building of the Palazzo Montalto, his private residence in Rome, to Fontana before he was elected pope. When Gregory XIII stripped the cardinal of his benefices, to show his displeasure at the cardinal's extravagance, Fontana lent Sixtus the money to keep building.

Examining the obelisk where it had been placed by Caligula, Fontana found that it was not exactly upright, but leaned toward the basilica by seventeen inches from the perpendicular. He set to work preparing the new site and the pope gave him carte blanche, ordering that any buildings that were in the way were to be demolished and that he was to take whatever he needed from just about anyone as long as it was paid for. Sixtus ordered all officials in Rome to "obey, favor, and assist him without delay or any manner of excuse notwithstanding any other commands whatever."

The project began on September 25, 1585, the anniversary of Sixtus having been appointed a bishop, with the construction of the foundation of the new site. That required a hole forty-five feet square and fifty-five feet deep.

Fontana ordered forty capstans to be built, to be manned by eight hundred men and seventy-five horses. Another 106 men were assigned to five levers. An apparatus, soon nicknamed Fontana's castello, or castle, ninety feet high was made of huge wooden beams, to act as both a scaffold and a crane, flanked the obelisk on two sides.*

The obelisk itself was encased in reed matting and two-inch-thick wood planks. This was covered in turn with vertical iron rods that were held in place by horizontal iron bands that provided places to attach pulley blocks. Ropes three inches thick and 750 feet long were ordered to be manufactured.

The weight of the obelisk had to be distributed evenly among the forty capstans, for if even one rope snapped, it

---

* While worker safety did not become a major concern until the twentieth century, Fontana required that all the men working on or near the scaffolding wear iron hard hats.

might prove disastrous. Fontana rehearsed the whole operation, using a trumpet to signal when the men and horses were to begin turning the capstans and a bell to single when they were to stop.

Finally, on November 16, 1585, everything was ready. Fontana had extra men standing by, along with additional supplies. Two masses were said before work began and "all officials, workers, master builders, and carters who were to assist in this great deed took communion."

A huge crowd assembled to watch the event, everyone from dukes to ambassadors to the pope's family (but not the pope himself). Every window and rooftop that had a view was crowded with people.

Fontana asked for all to kneel and pray and then the trumpet sounded and the vast array of men and horses was set in motion. The obelisk, slightly out of the vertical, straightened, and the castle let out a loud noise as the timbers took the weight of the stone. In twelve turns of the capstans, the obelisk was lifted "two palms" off its base.*

Underneath the obelisk were found several coins arranged in the shape of a cross. Some speculated that one of the workmen who had erected the obelisk nearly 1,550 years earlier had been a Christian. But seeing that the obelisk had been erected in Rome in A.D. 37 and Jesus had been crucified no more than seven years earlier, that seems highly unlikely. It was probably pure coincidence.

---

* In Rome, a palm was the length of the hand, not the width. The standard palm was about 8.25 inches.

Eight days later, the next and most dangerous step, lowering the obelisk onto the sledge, was ready to be attempted. Fontana had rearranged the capstans and had four attached to the obelisk's foot and pulleys attached to the now half-ruined sacristy of the old basilica to hold

Lowering the obelisk before moving it to St. Peter's Square.

it from above. On the signal, the four capstans attached to the foot began to move while the others slowly slacked off. Slowly it descended until it lay horizontal on the sledge.

As Fontana reported in the book he wrote on the project, "news of the success was received with infinite jubilation, and in recognition, the architect was accompanied with drums and trumpets to his home."*

With the obelisk down, the whole apparatus had to be carefully dismantled and moved to the new site, which was forty palms (about 27 feet) lower than the old site, but with the new pedestal, it was only three palms lower. Fontana had a ramp, 275 feet long, constructed, its sides reinforced with buttresses, so that when the obelisk arrived at the new site, it would be at the right height to be lifted onto the new pedestal.

Capstans pulled the obelisk along the ramp until it was in position to be raised, under the reerected wooden castello. On Wednesday, September 10, 1586, a full ten months later, at dawn, after two masses and everyone having taken communion, the obelisk began to rise. As the obelisk slowly settled onto the bronze supports on its new base, the weight slowly came off the ropes and the castello. A plumb line was used to determine if it was leaning at all and bronze shims were inserted under the bronze supports until it was absolutely vertical.

---

* In his book, Fontana referred to himself in the third person.

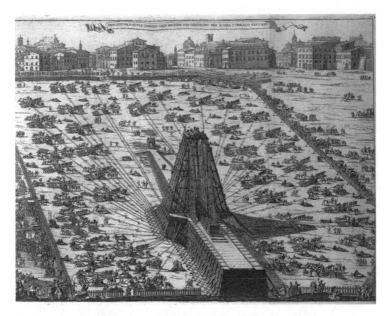

Pulling the obelisk into position in St. Peter's Square.

The operation was finally completed on September 26, 1586, a year and a day after it had begun. Sixtus V ordered a solemn ceremony to exorcize the obelisk of whatever pagan spirits might still be about it and to consecrate the cross that would be placed on its summit. "Half of Rome had gathered" to watch the ceremony, presided over by the pope himself.

On the south side of the base, an inscription proclaimed that the obelisk, which had been "dedicated to the wicked cult of heathen gods," had now been moved by Sixtus V "with great toil and labor into the precincts of the Apostles."

St. Peter's Square from the dome of St. Peter's.

Sixtus richly rewarded Fontana for his success with money, gold medallions, and the gift of all the materials used in the operation. He was also made a knight of the Golden Spur and given an annual pension of two thousand scudi, more than enough to live in considerable comfort. The entire cost of the operation was estimated at twenty thousand scudi.

Fontana worked for Sixtus V, using his castello to erect the other obelisks restored by Sixtus, until the pope's death in 1590. He afterward worked for Pope Clement VIII (reigned 1592–1605), but they fell out and Fontana was accused of misappropriating funds. He spent his last years in Naples, where he started the construction of the Palazzo Reale.*

BENITO MUSSOLINI, WHO dominated Italy from 1920 until 1943, never tired of emulating the Roman emperors and longed to restore the grandeur that had, long ago, been Rome. In 1932 he erected a monument to himself, in the Foro Mussolini, now the Foro Italico. It was, naturally enough, an obelisk. Quarried from Carrara marble, it stands seventeen meters high (a little over fifty-five feet), the largest piece of Carrara marble ever quarried. But it stands

---

* Sixtus's pontificate was followed by three of the shortest reigns in papal history. His successor, Urban VII, reigned for only twelve days, the shortest pontificate in history. Gregory XIV then reigned for 315 days. Gregory's successor, Innocent IX, reigned only sixty-two days before his death.

on a base of equal height, making it more than 110 feet tall altogether. Down the side are incised the words MUSSO-LINI DUX, "Mussolini the leader."

After World War Two, which ended in Italy with the dead Mussolini strung up by his heels in Milan, monuments and place names relating to fascism and Mussolini disappeared. But it was impossible to remove the deeply-incised MUSSOLINI DUX from the obelisk and base and it remains to this day the only public reference to the despised dictator in all of Italy.

Not content with building his own obelisk, Mussolini, like the emperors before him, also claimed an obelisk as a prize of war. In 1935 Italy invaded the empire of Ethiopia and seized control of the then poor and backward country. But that area had not always been poor. From about A.D. 100 to 900, the Axum Kingdom had flourished at the southern end of the Red Sea. Its geographic location was a nexus of trade routes that led north to Egypt and the Mediterranean world and east into Arabia and, across the Arabian Sea, to India. It also had trade routes reaching west and south into the interior of Africa.

At its height, the kingdom controlled not only what is now northern Ethiopia and Eritrea, but also western Yemen and southern Saudi Arabia. As it grew wealthy, the kings and nobles began marking their graves with ever-taller stelae, which were similar to obelisks although they were not topped with a pyramidion. The largest of these towered 107 feet in height before it fell. In late 1935 Italian soldiers found another stele that had stood seventy-nine feet high before it fell in the fourth century A.D., breaking into five pieces.

Mussolini ordered that it be transported to Rome. This was no easy task over the very poor roads of Ethiopia as the pieces of the obelisk weighed about 160 tons. But it was eventually hauled, piece by piece, to the port of Massawa in what is now Eritrea and shipped to Naples and then, by truck again, to Rome. Mussolini ordered it erected in Porta Capena Square, in front of what was then the Ministry for Italian Africa.

In 1947 Italy agreed with the United Nations to return the stela, along with the Lion of Judah statue that had long symbolized the country of Ethiopia. But while the statue was returned in 1967, not until 2005 was the stela dismantled into three pieces and shipped out of Italy to be reerected in 2008 in Axum, which had been the capital of the Axum Kingdom.

There were three ways to get the stela back to where it belonged. The first was by sea, through the port of Massawa in Eritrea, the opposite of its trip to Italy. But relations between Eritrea and Ethiopia, which is landlocked, were at a low point, so this route was politically impossible. The second was via the big international airport in Addis Ababa, the capital of Ethiopia. But while there were planes capable of carrying the three pieces one at a time, the roads between Addis Ababa and Axum were not up to handling trucks capable of such weights.

The only alternative was to lengthen the runway at the airport in Axum, which took considerable time. Finally, in

April 2005, the Italian government, using an Antonov AN-124, the world's largest production cargo plane, delivered the first of the three sections, the heaviest and largest piece of air cargo ever carried.

Three more years passed before the stela was reerected, but it stands today, the only stolen obelisk ever to be returned to its country of origin. It is likely to remain the only one for the foreseeable future.

CHAPTER FIVE

Paris and London Take Their Prizes

JUST AS OCTAVIAN and Antony fought in Egypt for the mastery of the Roman Empire 1,800 years earlier, so Britain and France fought there for the mastery of Europe in the great conflict known as the Napoleonic Wars. And, like Octavian, each of the contestants would bring home obelisks.

Napoleon was nothing if not audacious. Lacking the means to attack Great Britain directly, he decided to do so indirectly by conquering Egypt.* That would establish a

---

* As Admiral Lord St. Vincent famously said in the House of Lords when challenged as to the possibility of a French invasion, "I did not say they cannot come, I only said they cannot come by sea." This prompted a cartoon in a British newspaper, showing Napoleon invading Britain by means of Montgolfier balloons.

French presence in the Middle East and provide a gateway to India, which, in turn, would threaten British possessions there by linking up with Tipu Sultan, the ruler of Mysore and an enemy of the British.

But, typical of Napoleon, he also intended to mount a major scientific and cultural expedition to explore Egypt and its ancient past. When he invaded on July 1, 1798, with an army of forty thousand men, he also took 167 scientists, including naturalists, linguists, geologists, mathematicians, and archeologists.*

Napoleon managed to evade the Royal Navy and get his army to Egypt. There, the Mamelukes, a military caste that, nominally slaves of the Ottoman Sultan, ruled Egypt, proved to be no match for a modern, well-equipped army. With the Battle of the Pyramids, where the French suffered three hundred casualties and the Mamelukes six thousand, Egypt fell into Napoleon's hands.†

But then, eleven days later, Admiral Horatio Nelson, who had been searching for the French fleet for weeks, finally found them at Aboukir Bay, east of Alexandria, in a strong defensive position. The French admiral believed that

---

*The most spectacular find of this groups of savants, as they were known, was the Rosetta Stone. Carved in 196 B.C., when Egypt was ruled by the Ptolemies, a Greek dynasty founded by one of Alexander the Great's generals, it was a public display of a decree that was written in ancient Greek, demotic (the form of the ancient Egyptian language that used a simplified alphabet; modern Coptic developed out of it), and hieroglyphics. It proved to be the key to understanding hieroglyphic writing, which had previously been completely untranslatable.

† Like many battles, the Battle of the Pyramids is misnamed. It took place about nine miles from Giza, and the pyramids were not even in sight from the battlefield.

his anchored fleet could only be attacked from the sea, confident that the British ships would not be able to get between the French fleet and the land. He underestimated British confidence in their own seamanship.

At six twenty in the evening of August 1, the British attacked and soon sailed both to landward and seaward of the French fleet, which came under very heavy cross fire. Eighteenth-century warships did not have enough crew to man the guns of both sides at one time, and the utter destruction of the French fleet began. By nine o'clock, much of that fleet had surrendered or been destroyed and the flagship, *L'Orient*, was on fire. At ten o'clock, the fire reached the magazine and a titanic explosion ripped the great three-decker apart, spreading debris up to five hundred yards away and killing eight hundred of her thousand-man crew.

Of the thirteen ships in the French fleet, eleven were captured or destroyed. French casualties were about thirty-five hundred, while British wounded and dead amounted to about nine hundred. The Battle of the Nile, as it came to be called, was the first of the three great victories that would elevate Nelson above all other admirals in naval history.*

The most immediate effect of the battle was to trap Napoleon and his army in Egypt, for Nelson's victory had made the Mediterranean a British lake. Napoleon managed to escape on a French frigate in August 1799, but the British

---

* The others were Copenhagen (1801) and Trafalgar (1805).

army that landed in Egypt in 1801 along with Ottoman forces defeated the French, who then had no option but capitulation. The British agreed to repatriate what was left of the French army in British ships.

Among the spoils of war that fell to the British was the vast hoard of antiquities collected by the French scientists, which is why the Rosetta Stone is today in the British Museum and not the Louvre.

WHILE THE FRENCH expedition to Egypt was a total military failure, it was a scientific triumph. In 1809, the first volume of the *Description de l'Égypte* was published in Paris, the fruit of the scientists whom Napoleon had taken to Egypt with him. Over the next twenty years, these immense volumes (they measure 39 inches by 34 inches) were published one by one. In all there are twenty volumes in the first edition, ten text volumes and ten volumes of plates, 894 plates in all, made from more than three thousand drawings.

While it was not the first work of Egyptology, it was certainly the most massive and it caused a sort of Egyptomania—and not in France alone. Egyptian-inspired jewelry and hairstyles became fashionable in Europe and America, as did neo-Egyptian architecture. Manhattan's municipal jail is still called "The Tombs" after the nickname of a neo-Egyptian predecessor built in 1838. The craze also made both the British and French governments want obelisks to decorate their capital cities.

Napoleon is supposed to have wanted to take an obelisk to Paris and, at least according to legend, Josephine's parting words to him before he left for Egypt, were "Goodbye! If you get to Thebes, do send me a little obelisk." As Britain controlled the Mediterranean, there was no possibility of an obelisk while Napoleon reigned as emperor. But after his abdication in 1814, the restored King Louis XVIII asked his consul general in Alexandria to approach Muhammad Ali Pasha, who ruled Egypt at that point, about being given one.

Muhammad Ali (1769–1849) is often regarded as the father of modern Egypt. An ethnic Albanian, he was born a

Muhammad Ali Pasha.

subject of the Ottoman Sultan and in 1801 was sent to Egypt as part of the army that landed in Aboukir Bay to recover Egypt for the sultan from French control. A master politician, he cultivated the people, destroyed the remaining power of the Mamelukes, already seriously weakened by Napoleon, and proclaimed himself khedive, effectively the ruler of Egypt, although nominally the sultan's viceroy.*

Muhammad Ali, who didn't care at all about Egypt's antiquities, was happy to present one of the two obelisks that Augustus had transported from Heliopolis to Alexandria to the French and the other one to the British.† Because he was technically only the governor of an Ottoman province, Muhammad Ali could not exchange ambassadors with other countries, so one way of gaining favor was to send them obelisks instead.

Nothing further happened with the monuments until 1829, by which time King Charles X was on the throne of France.

Jean-François Champollion, a noted Egyptologist and linguist, thought the Alexandria obelisks were uninspiring and that France should ask Muhammad Ali for the two obelisks at Luxor. Muhammad Ali had already promised them to the British, and so the French worked out a deal with Mohammad Ali. They would get the Luxor obelisks

---

* In 1811, Muhammad Ali invited the Mameluke leaders to a celebration in the Cairo Citadel in honor of his son, Tusan, who was about to set off on a military expedition. When the leaders had assembled, Ali's troops massacred them to a man. He then systematically defeated the remaining Mameluke forces around the country.
† The French one would eventually come to New York's Central Park. See Chapter Seven.

and the British would get the great obelisk at Karnak, the biggest of all obelisks. The French were playing a trick, however, because they knew that the Karnak obelisk could not be moved without destroying the entire temple and the British were very unlikely to do that, as, indeed, they did not.

Champollion (1790–1832) was born in the small town of Figeac in southern France in humble circumstances (his father was the town drunk). But he soon showed extraordinary talents, especially in languages, and a fascination with Egypt. He first studied Latin and Greek, but quickly mastered Hebrew, Arabic, Syriac, Persian, and Coptic as well.

Jean-François Champollion.

Apparently Joseph Fourier, a mathematician and Egyptologist who had accompanied Napoleon to Egypt and had been entrusted by him with the editorship of the *Description*, heard about Champollion and invited him to his house in Grenoble, where the boy, only eleven, was enthralled with his collection of Egyptian artifacts. According to legend, when told that the hieroglyphics were undecipherable, Champollion said that he would be the one to do it.

Twenty-one years later, he did. Many thought that hieroglyphics were mystical symbols and thus inherently untranslatable, but Champollion was sure they were at least semi-alphabetical. It had long been suggested that hiero-glyphics enclosed in ovals—cartouches—represented the names of pharaohs. Champollion deciphered a cartouche on the Rosetta Stone as spelling out "Ptolemy," but got no further. Then, in 1819, an obelisk provided the vital clue. The antiquarian and Egyptologist (and intimate friend of the poet Lord Byron) William John Bankes noticed that the small obelisk he had brought back to England, the so-called Philae obelisk, had the names of both Ptolemy and Cleopatra written on it in Greek.* It also bore a cartouche of what was thought to be Ptolemy and another cartouche.

What Champollion thought were the symbols for "p," "o," and "l" in the Ptolemy cartouche were in exactly the

---

* This was Cleopatra, the Queen of Ptolomy IX, not the later and far more famous Cleopatra VII.

Obelisk at Sir William Bankes' estate at Kingston Lacy in England.

right places to spell out "Cleopatra" in the other cartouche. That cartouche, in turn, provided other symbols and Champollion soon cracked the code. He then demonstrated that hieroglyphics from earlier periods, such as the obelisks created in the New Kingdom, were also alphabetic in nature. Obelisks, then, proved to be essential to opening the window into the language of ancient Egypt and thus into Egypt's long, rich history.*

---

* The Rosetta space mission, launched by the European Space Agency in 2004 to be the first space probe to orbit a comet, launched a further probe to actually land on the comet, which it successfully did on November 12, 2014. The name of the lander is Philae, in honor of William Bankes' obelisk.

In 1824 he published his *Précis du Système Hiéro-glyphique*, which included a grammar of ancient Egyptian and his decipherment of the various hieroglyphic symbols. While controversial at first, Champollion's accomplishment has long been accepted as one of the great cryptographic and philological accomplishments of all time and he is one of the founders of the science of Egyptology.

In 1828, Champollion led a scientific expedition to Egypt. While there he tried to convince the khedive to give France the two obelisks at Luxor in place of the one at Alexandria. The trip ruined his always very fragile health and, back in Paris, he died of a stroke at the age of forty-one. He lies today in Père Lachaise cemetery in Paris, his grave marked, appropriately, by an obelisk.

In 1829, the French navy minister asked the king for permission to proceed with securing one of the obelisks the khedive had given France and sent Baron Isidore Taylor to negotiate the final details. Taylor, whose father had been born in Britain and had taken French citizenship, was a distinguished writer and indefatigable traveler and art collector, and he had convinced the khedive to give France the Luxor obelisks.

Once title was fully in hand, the navy began construction of a ship designed to transport an obelisk out of Egypt for the first time in 1,500 years. And this time, the vessel needed to do more than just make it across the Mediterranean. As Lieutenant Seaton Schroeder, a U.S. Navy engineer and second in command of moving New York's obelisk half a century later, explained,

The *Luxor* was an immense barge [by which he meant flat-bottomed] of such build as to ascend the Nile, receive on board one of the obelisks, and bring it to Paris. That is to say, the task set the constructors was to produce a vessel that could navigate two rivers and the high seas, should not draw more than six and a half feet with the obelisk in, should pass under the bridges across the Seine, and should be strong enough to take the enormous weight while lying on a beach. Of course M. Rolland [the architect] had to depart from the usual rules of naval architecture; the proportion of length to breadth was very small, five keels were fitted, and the necessary longitudinal and transverse strength obtained by multiplying fastenings and ties. The result was an immensely strong craft, shaped like a parallelopipedon [a solid whose bases are parallelograms]; three masts were given her.

Not surprisingly, the *Luxor* was a very poor sailor. "The novel craft behaved at sea much as might be expected; with a fair wind she made as much as eight knots, but when close-hauled her progress was crab-like."

As soon as the ship was launched, however, the July Revolution of 1830 broke out. Charles X abdicated and Louis-Philippe took the throne as "King of the French" as opposed to his predecessor's title "King of France."* The

---

*This distinction continues today even with the French monarchy long gone. François Hollande is not, technically, "Président de France," but "le Président de la République Française."

khedive didn't care a whit who sat on the French throne and confirmed the gift.

The *Luxor* arrived in Alexandria on May 3, 1831. A marine engineer, Jean-Baptiste Apollinaire Lebas, was appointed in charge of the operation and on June 8 he and the French consul general met with the khedive. Lebas was notably short (as his surname inadvertently suggests) and the khedive couldn't resist a joke at his expense. As Lebas reported in his diary,

> The governor [Muhammad Ali] who knew beforehand of my short stature, pretended not to have seen me when I was presented to him by the consul-general and asked, "But where is your engineer? Tell him to sit beside me so that I may see him."

THE *LUXOR* BEGAN her journey up the Nile from Alexandria on June 11, 1831, and did not reach Luxor until August 13. The annual flood had begun and time was of the essence. The stonecutter who was part of the expedition quickly ascertained that the obelisk was cracked. He thought, however, that it could remain intact, "if it falls softly, very softly."

Fortunately, the crack was not serious. Once the obelisk was tilted off the vertical it was found that mortises had been chiseled into either side of the crack and filled with what had once been wooden dogs shaped like bow ties to prevent the crack from widening. The wood had, of course, long turned to dust.

Thirty houses had to be demolished to lower and move the obelisk, and at first the owners flatly refused to sell. When the governor of Upper Egypt was informed, he sent his interpreter and a guardsman. "Those two worthies," Lieutenant Schroeder recounted decades later, "naturally proposed to end the matter *à la Turque*, but were persuaded to desist, and a commission was appointed to appraise the buildings and decide the amount to be paid each proprietor." The houses surrounded, and were inside of, the temple of Karnak, which suffered considerable damage in the process of tearing down the houses. In addition, fifty thousand cubic yards of dirt and stone had to be removed— all hauled by human labor—to make a causeway down to the Nile.

Lebas decided to lower the obelisk onto the side facing the river, making it easier to haul down to the *Luxor*, which would be about 430 yards away, aground once the flood season ended.

A scaffold was erected in order to sheath the obelisk in planking to protect it during the lowering, shipping, and reerecting. But as soon as that task was accomplished, on September 1, cholera broke out. Many of the Arab workmen died on the job and it took a month before the sheathing alone was completed.

Unlike Fontana 245 years earlier, Lebas did not erect a "castle," but instead, perhaps because he was a marine engineer, used multiple sheers—cranes often used in shipyards for lifting heavy objects into and out of ships. Rope six and a quarter inches in diameter and pulleys were attached to capstans with sixteen bars, each to be powered by four men.

On October 24 at dawn, the operation began. But when the obelisk was eight degrees from the vertical, the movement ceased and the officer in charge of the capstans told Lebas that the capstans' anchors were dragging in the sand. Lebas ordered that the slacking ropes be let loose more easily and the rotary motion began again and the obelisk was soon at an angle of twenty-five degrees.

It took several days to lower the obelisk to the horizontal. At one point the motion stopped entirely and no amount of force would get it moving again; some of the wood had sagged under the strain and earth had to be dug out from underneath the base of the obelisk, a nerve-wracking procedure at best. When force was again applied, the obelisk lurched forward three feet and stuck again. The procedure had to be done again and again, but, finally, on November 16, the obelisk was horizontal and on the causeway that led to the *Luxor*, now aground at the edge of the Nile.

Another month of backbreaking effort was required to get it to the *Luxor*. Once the obelisk was in position, the bow of the Luxor had to be sawed off to allow the obelisk to be hauled aboard, an operation that, for once, went like clockwork. And in only two hours on December 19, the monolith was aboard the *Luxor*, which was soon repaired and ready to sail, except for the fact that it was hard aground and would not float again until the flood began the following August. So for eight long months Lebas and his team cooled their heels in Luxor.

Finally, on August 18, 1832, the *Luxor* floated and a week later began its journey down the Nile to Alexandria. They anchored every night so progress was slow, and by the time they reached Rosetta, on October 1, at the mouth of the westernmost branch of the river, just east of Aboukir Bay, the water had fallen and the level over the sandbar was too shallow for the *Luxor* to make it through. Everyone concerned expected to wait out the winter and spring at Rosetta, until the Nile rose again.

But then a fortuitous accident to another ship solved the problem. A bark carrying oranges had sunk in the pass and in the process of raising her, a way was opened for the *Luxor*, which made it through on the evening of January 1, 1833. From there she was towed by the French paddle-wheel steamer *Sphinx* to Alexandria. Bad weather delayed her there until April 1, when she and the *Sphinx* set off for Toulon, the great French naval base east of Marseille.

She had a stormy passage across the Mediterranean and her captain had to seek shelter in numerous ports on the Mediterranean's northern littoral along the way, much as the obelisk ships of the Roman era had. Arriving finally at Toulon on May 10, the ungainly ship had to undergo a month's quarantine in Toulon. The journey around the Iberian Peninsula, north to the English Channel, and then up the Seine took another six months and she reached Paris, still under tow, December 23. But then, the opposite of their sojourn on the banks of the Nile, the crew had to wait for the Seine to fall and not until August 1834 was the obelisk hauled out of the *Luxor*.

It then had to wait again, as, strangely, no one had thought about the pedestal that it was to be put on. A further two years passed before the pedestal was designed, quarried, finished, and brought to Paris. Finally, all was ready to erect the obelisk in the Place de la Concorde. Initially a steam engine, regarded in 1836 as the greatest wonder of the modern age, was intended to replace the muscle power of men multiplied by capstans and pulleys. But the engine broke down in trials. As the *Journal des Débats* reported on October 16, 1836,

> It is much to be regretted that sufficient precautions were not taken to ensure this engine working satisfactorily. The idea of inaugurating the steam engine on so solemn an occasion was most happy .... It would have been well to associate the monuments of antique art with the finest productions of the inventive mind of modern times. It would have been well to show 200,000 people one of these engines, ... seizing the obelisk of Sesostris,* and raising it little by little with perfect regularity of motion, without the aid of a living being, ... These machines are destined to relieve man of all work that needs only brute force, and even much, such is their perfection, of some work that may seem to demand guidance from an intelligent being. The

---

* Sesostris, who is mentioned in Herodotus as a pharaoh who had conquered as far as modern Bulgaria, was probably a semi-mythical figure concocted out of several real pharaohs, none of whom even reached Asia Minor, let alone Europe. The obelisk of Luxor, according to its hieroglyphic inscriptions, was ordered by Rameses II.

steam-engine . . . is nature enslaved; and it is the only slave, the only serf of the future.

When the obelisk was finally hauled to the pedestal, only five hours were needed to pull it up the final, heavily greased ramp in jerks of two or three feet at a time until it was only one inch from its final position. The ropes were stretched taut and the capstans stopped. With the obelisk under great strain from the ropes, two slight ramming blows were all that was needed to get the seventy-five-foot long, 275-ton obelisk exactly into place, ready to be raised to the vertical.

On October 25, 1836, more than five years after Lebas first went to Egypt to fetch an obelisk for Paris, all was

Erecting the obelisk from Egypt in the Place de la Concorde in Paris, October 25, 1836.

ready. A cedar box containing the then-current coinage of France, two medals with the image of the king on them, and an inscription that read, "*Sous le règne de Louis Philippe I, roi des français, M. De Gasparin tant ministre de l'intérieur, l'obélisque de 'Luxor' a été elévé sur son piédestal le 25 octobre, 1836, par les soins de M. Apollinaire LeBas, ingénieur de la marine*" was placed in a cavity in the pedestal.

At eleven thirty, two hundred thousand people crowded into the Place de la Concorde to watch (the total population of Paris in 1830 was 785,000). Lebas, stationed on the ledge of the pedestal, ordered the operation to begin. A bugle sounded and a company of artillerymen began turning the capstans. The point of the obelisk began to rise into the sky. At noon, to great cheers, the king and queen appeared at the windows of the naval ministry—effectively a front-row seat.

The operation continued until a cracking noise was heard, caused only by the great compression of the apparatus, which was practically the same as had been used to lower the obelisk in Egypt. Lebas ordered the operation to continue, only faster, as he wanted to get beyond the forty-five degree point, when the strain on the pedestal would be at its greatest point. Because of that strain it had been reenforced on the side away from the obelisk with heavy timbers to prevent it from moving.

Then someone noticed that the chains attached to the pyramidion to keep the obelisk from going past the vertical had been "stopped" to keep them out of the way as the ropes were rigged. But no one had thought to remove the stops, which, not designed to withstand strain, would have suddenly snapped and possibly caused a dangerous vibration. Two sailors scrambled up the obelisk and removed the stops.

The operation began again and at three o'clock, to an enormous roar from the crowd, the obelisk stood atop its pedestal, where it stands to this day. That night, fireworks were set off and the king gave three thousand francs to be distributed among the workers.

It was a singular feat of engineering. Fontana had had to lower and raise an obelisk, but he only had to move it a few hundred yards. Lebas had to move the Paris obelisk several thousand miles between its lowering and reerection. In honor of the feat, one side of the pedestal has the machinery designed by Lebas engraved on a plaque.

THE BRITISH TOOK a great deal longer to claim possession of their obelisk. At the Battle of Alexandria, March 21, 1801, between the French army and the newly landed British army, the latter's commander, Sir Ralph Abercromby, was fatally wounded. After the French surrender in September, it was proposed that the obelisk lying prone near the shore in Alexandria be taken to England and erected as a memorial to him and to the victory of British forces in Egypt. The officers and men subscribed no less than seven thousand pounds to bring this about and Lord Cavan, who had succeeded Abercromby in command, approved of the idea.

Major Alexander Bryce of the Royal Engineers devised a plan to raise a sunken French frigate and to build a pier out into the harbor where the obelisk could be loaded onto the ship. The pier was partially built but a storm swept it away and the army moved on, so the project was abandoned.

In 1819, the British consul in Alexandria reported that Muhammad Ali wanted to make a present to the prince regent, who would become King George IV the next year, in thanks for a corvette that had been transferred to the Egyptian navy. The consul suggested one of the Alexandria obelisks would "be considered a valuable addition to the embellishments designed for the British metropolis." The khedive soon agreed and specified that the obelisk lying on the ground was the one he was giving to England.

But again, nothing was done to actually take possession. In 1832, Parliament debated removing the obelisk but no money was appropriated. Thirty years later still, a suggestion was made to erect the obelisk in Hyde Park as a memorial to Prince Albert, who had recently died and had been the major force behind creating the Great Exhibition of 1851, the first world's fair, housed in the Crystal Palace in Hyde Park. Again, this led nowhere.

Fraser's Magazine, a leading London publication in the mid-nineteenth century, wrote that "England appears from her apparent bewilderment in the matter, to be in the position of the elderly lady who won an elephant in the lottery."

Finally General Sir James Alexander, struck by the obelisk in the Place de la Concorde, determined to finally bring the British obelisk in Alexandria to London.

Alexander (1803–85) lived a life that could only have been lived in the Victorian era. Born in Scotland, he joined the East India Company in 1820 and transferred to the British Army in 1825. He witnessed or fought in wars from Portugal to the Balkans to Persia to South Africa to the Crimea to New Zealand. He led scientific expeditions to Africa and cofounded the Royal Geographical Society. He wrote fourteen books, from travel narratives to a

Gen. Sir James Edward Alexander.

two-volume biography of the Duke of Wellington to a guide to salmon fishing in Canada.

In 1875 he went to Egypt with an introduction from the Earl of Derby, then the foreign secretary, to the British consul general in Alexandria. The consul arranged a meeting with the then reigning khedive, who reaffirmed the gift.

When he got back to England he prepared to raise the necessary financing in London's City, as Parliament was not inclined to foot the bill. But when he talked about it with his friend Erasmus Wilson, the latter offered to pay for the entire expense.*

With the khedive's permission and the necessary funds in hand, a plan had to be devised to get the obelisk to England and erect it. As usual, there were no end of suggestions. One man somewhat ingeniously proposed encasing the obelisk in a cylinder of wood sufficient to float the stone and then roll it down into the Mediterranean. There it would be slung between two steamers, being carried underwater to lower its weight by a little less than half.

In January 1877, Erasmus Wilson signed a contract with John Dixon, a civil engineer, agreeing to pay him ten

---

* Wilson was a distinguished surgeon and dermatologist, knighted by Queen Victoria in 1881. He made a fortune from his practice and very shrewd investments. Childless, he was a notable benefactor, endowing professorships and paying for the large medical library in the Hunterian Museum in London. After his wife's death, his £200,000 estate, a vast sum for the time, went to the Royal College of Surgeons. He is also famous for a less-than-accurate prediction in 1878 when he said that "When the Paris Exhibition closes, electric light will close with it and no more be heard of."

thousand pounds once the obelisk was erected, with Dixon to assume all risk.

Because the shore near where the obelisk lay had shoals and was exposed to gales, no oceangoing ship capable of handling the obelisk could be safely anchored there. Either a special vessel would need to be built that could deal with the problem, or the obelisk would have to be transported through the streets of Alexandria to the harbor.

Dixon decided to build a vessel in England and ship it, in pieces, to Egypt. It would be cylindrical and thus, once built around the obelisk, could be rolled into the sea and then out to where it could be towed by an oceangoing ship.

This was no easy matter. As Lieutenant Schroeder explained in an appendix he wrote for a history of the New York obelisk, "The design of a vessel is generally made to meet the requirements of the service on which she will be employed at sea. In this particular case, however, the builders had the novel experience of constructing a seaworthy craft in which everything had to be subordinated to the one prime feature that would enable her to be launched by rolling down the beach."

But if the center of gravity of the obelisk were to coincide with the center of gravity of the vessel, once the vessel started to roll, it would, thanks to its mass, keep on doing so, impeded only by the friction with the water. In other words it would continue to roll almost indefinitely. Thus the obelisk had to be centered four inches below the center of gravity of the vessel as a whole and an additional five inches were achieved with iron ballast. To reduce the pitching motion as much as possible, the fat end of the obelisk was to be placed in the bow, and thus the center of gravity was nearer the bow.

The work of construction was entrusted to the Thames Ironworks. The length of the vessel, dubbed *Cleopatra*, was ninety-three feet, with a diameter of fifteen feet. She was divided into ten watertight compartments. To prevent the obelisk from breaking due to any flexing of the vessel in rough weather, elastic timber cushions were provided that allowed the *Cleopatra* to flex up to five inches without the obelisk being affected, far above any calculated deflection.

The obelisk is sixty-eight feet, five and one half inches long, plus another seven feet six inches for the pyramidion. The weight is about 186 tons. When work began in early June 1877, the accumulated sand and debris was cleared

Design of the ship *Cleopatra* that brought the obelisk from Egypt to London.

from the obelisk and the large timbers placed under it. Hydraulic jacks (which had not been available to Apollinaire Lebas) were used to skew it around so that it was parallel to the shore.

When the ground was seen to sag under its weight, an underground vault was discovered, containing two skulls, several arm and leg bones, and several small jars that contained only dust. The skulls were put on board the *Cleopatra* before she sailed, but were never seen again.

As the *Cleopatra* was built up around the stone, the way to the sea was graded and the sea wall demolished. Numerous blocks of stone had to be removed from the sea floor, many of them with elaborate hieroglyphics, indicating great age. Farther out a large wall was encountered, constructed of blocks that weighed as much as twenty tons. It was demolished with dynamite, another technology unavailable to Lebas, having been invented by Alfred Nobel and patented only in 1867.

Afraid that rocks just below the bottom of the sea would be exposed when the cylinder rolled over them, engineers constructed two rings of wood, nine inches thick, around the cylinder near the bow and stern to act as wheels and keep the skin of the *Cleopatra* away from the bottom itself.

On August 28, all was finally ready. Wire hawsers were wrapped around the *Cleopatra* and attached to lighters out at sea. Other hawsers were attached on the land side to prevent the cylinder from moving too fast. Four powerful steam jacks were placed against the side of the cylinder and the operation began at six A.M. *Cleopatra* rolled very slowly at first, so slowly in fact that it had made only one revolution by noon, about fifty feet. The wire hawsers attached to the lighters proved useless as the lighters' anchors dragged in the poor holding ground. Ropes were taken out to two steam tugs that, steaming at full power, could just keep the *Cleopatra* moving.

By five thirty that evening it had reached the water's edge. The planking that had been laid ended there and the incline became steeper. The cylinder rolled forward but then checked itself again and the slow progress resumed. Then, about seven o'clock, the cylinder took a sudden half turn and lay in about three feet of water.

Two mornings later, with little progress made, Dixon was horrified to discover that the vessel, not nearly as buoyant as it should have been, was apparently half full of water. Worse, the top side was, at that point, on the bottom and so the hatch could not be opened to see what was going on inside. A hole was opened on the exposed hull and a pump started, but it did not change the water level in the least. Obviously the vessel was leaking badly.

A diver was sent down and delivered the news that a large rock, hidden in the sand, had punctured the hull. Despite the carefully engineered watertight compartments, the entire vessel had filled with water. John Dixon later explained why:

> Now I shall never be hard, and can never be severe,
> on any naval captains, or anyone else after what

occurred. There were six or seven of us with every inducement to pay every attention to that vessel. There was Mr. Waynman Dixon in actual charge of the operations, the others looking on. We had provided bulkheads, we had provided watertight doors through them, and we had so carefully managed that the man whose duty it was to close those doors had forgotten to do so, and were all left open!

It required several days to remove the rock, which weighed about half a ton. Then the hole, which measured eighteen inches across, had to be patched with a plate, and the water pumped out. Finally on September 7, the tugs were called back and the cylinder was soon seen to be bobbing up and down in the swell, afloat at last.

The wooden "wheels" were stripped off, and the *Cleopatra* was towed around to the harbor. Put in a floating dock, bilge keels were attached, as was a cabin, bridge, and a mast for sails.* Finally, the rudder was hung. The *Cleopatra*, having been until now an iron caisson, had become, at least in theory, a ship. Twenty tons of iron ballast were placed in the bilge to help steady her further and she was ready for sea.

On September 21, under tow by the steamer *Olga*, the obelisk set off for England. The *Olga* stopped at Algiers and Gibraltar and then, on October 10, rounded

---

*The sails were not for locomotion, but merely to reduce rolling and make steering easier.

Cape Saint Vincent at the southwest tip of Portugal in fair weather.

While it was fair weather, it wasn't easy dealing with so peculiar a vessel. The *Cleopatra*'s captain, Henry Carter, inspected the vessel for leaks every six hours. To do so, he had to slip down through a hatch in his tiny cabin and then, holding a candle in his teeth, open a hatch in each watertight bulkhead, and pull himself through. Once the candle began to burn his nose and it went out when he dropped it. He had to feel his way back in the pitch dark. Thereafter he took a crewman with him to hold the candle.

By October 14, when the *Olga* and *Cleopatra* entered the notoriously stormy Bay of Biscay, to the north of Spain and to the west of France, the weather had deteriorated into a howling gale from the south-southwest.

The poor sailing qualities of the *Cleopatra* now became painfully apparent. Difficult to steer in calm weather, she yawed widely, straining the tow rope. As she lumbered in the waves, they frequently broke over her and threatened to wash the superstructure overboard.

Captain Carter decided to cast off from the *Olga* and ride to a sea anchor until the storm passed. He signaled *Olga* to cast off, but before this could happen, a big wave broke over the *Cleopatra* with such force that the ballast—which, it turned out, had not been properly secured—shifted and the *Cleopatra* rolled over onto her beam ends and stayed there.

There was no way to secure the ballast in these conditions and Carter decided there was no alternative but to abandon ship. The *Cleopatra*'s lifeboat was lowered but was immediately smashed to pieces against the rudder. The captain of the *Olga* saw what had happened and asked for volunteers to go to the rescue. Six sailors manned one of the *Olga*'s lifeboats and got safely away from that ship. But as they approached the *Cleopatra*, a wave broke over them and neither they nor the lifeboat was ever seen again.*

Captain Booth managed to get a line to the *Cleopatra* and a boat was hauled alongside. Carter and his crew finally reached the safety of the *Olga*. The tow was cast off and Booth went in search of the lost sailors. After the fruitless search, Booth was unable to find the *Cleopatra* and decided that she must have foundered. He set a course for Falmouth, near Land's End in Cornwall.

But the *Cleopatra* had not foundered. She was sighted the next day by another British steamer, the *Fitzmaurice*. Taken in tow, the *Cleopatra* was brought to the Spanish port of Ferrol, at the northwest corner of the Iberian Peninsula. The owners of the *Fitzmaurice,* knowing the value of the obelisk, put in a claim for salvage in the amount of five thousand pounds. The Spanish admiralty court, which had jurisdiction, knocked this down to two thousand pounds, one thousand to the owners, two hundred fifty to the captain of the *Fitzmaurice*, and seven hundred fifty to be divided among the crew.

---

* At Queen Victoria's suggestion, their names were listed on a plaque on one side of the pedestal of the obelisk.

That sum was still a large one, at a time when two hundred pounds a year was a middle-class income. And as Dixon's contract with Erasmus Wilson called for Dixon to bear all risks, Dixon's hopes of a profit were gone and worse.

The *Cleopatra*, now towed by the tug *Anglia*, finally reached the Thames on January 20, 1878.

The London newspapers had been consumed with "the battle of the sites," over where, exactly, to erect the obelisk. Locations in St. James's Park, near Greenwich Hospital, along Horse Guards Parade, in Green Park, in front of the British Museum, and in Regent Circus, all had their adherents. Dixon wanted it erected near Westminster Abbey and statues of Sir Robert Peel, Lord Derby, and Lord Palmerston, former prime ministers. He even

THE CYLINDER SHIP CLEOPATRA, WITH THE OBELISK, AT WESTMINSTER BRIDGE.

The *Cleopatra* arriving in London at Westminster Bridge on January 20, 1878.

erected a wooden model of the obelisk there to show how it would look.

But the authorities at the underground Metropolitan Railway were worried about their tunnel that ran underneath the site and demanded a perpetual indemnity against the possibility of the obelisk breaking through and crashing down into the tunnel.

The Metropolitan Board of Works, which had the final say in the matter, was reluctant to have the obelisk moved through the London streets, for fear that its weight might adversely impact the new sewer and water pipes that had been recently laid and had done so much to clean up London's dreadful water pollution problems. It decided on a site on the Thames Embankment, between Waterloo Bridge and Charing Cross Bridge (now usually known as Hungerford Railroad Bridge).

From an engineering standpoint it was by far the easiest site to deal with as the obelisk could be brought by water right up to it, with no ground transportation required at all. However, the site is a bit removed from the heart of ceremonial London, with the Houses of Parliament and Buckingham Palace, to the west.

The vaults of the embankment were filled in with concrete and a concrete base, lying on the hard clay beneath the muck at the bottom of the Thames, was provided.

The *Cleopatra* was brought up to the site and grounded at high tide on a wooden cradle. Her superstructure was removed and she was given a quarter turn so that the best face of the obelisk was toward the roadway. The *Cleopatra* was then dismantled, her one and only voyage—an adventurous one, to be sure—at an end. Dixon used hydraulic jacks to lift the obelisk up to the embankment and screw jacks pushed her to where the center of gravity of the obelisk was exactly over the spot where the pedestal would be erected.

Dixon then erected a "castle" not dissimilar to the castle used by Fontana three centuries earlier. A wrought-iron jacket was placed around the obelisk's center of gravity, cushioned by wood and twenty feet long to assure that the weight of the two ends of the obelisk did not cause the obelisk to crack while being lifted.

As the hydraulic jacks lifted the obelisk, timber blocking was built up as it rose to ensure that any failure of the jacks would not result in the obelisk falling. As the

Rasing the obelisk in London, August, 1878.

obelisk lay hovering horizontally above in its wrought-iron jacket, the pedestal was constructed below.

Inevitably a time capsule was placed in the pedestal, containing such things as standard weights and measures and a set of British coinage including an Empress of India rupee along with Queen Victoria's portrait.* More quotidian items were also included, such as a case of cigars, a box of hairpins, photographs of a dozen women regarded as especially beautiful, a razor, a railway guide, *Whitaker's Almanack*, a baby bottle, and children's toys. Wire ropes and sections of marine cables were added[†] with Bibles in several languages, a Hebrew Torah, and verse sixteen of chapter three of the Gospel of Saint John translated into 215 languages.[‡]

On September 11, 1878, the pedestal being complete, the apparatus was tested and found to be working properly. The next day, at three P.M., a large crowd assembled on both sides of the river and the obelisk, adorned with British and Turkish flags, was turned vertical in only half an hour. The next day it was set down on the pedestal and Great Britain had her obelisk.

The obelisk was soon flanked with large bronze sphinxes, nineteen feet long and weighing seven tons

---

* Queen Victoria had been proclaimed Empress of India two years earlier, in 1876.

[†] The Atlantic Cable had been successfully laid in 1866 and was still considered one of the wonders of the modern world. Undersea cables were rapidly spreading around the world at this time, shrinking the globe by an order of magnitude.

[‡] "For God so loved the world, that he gave his only begotten Son, that whosoever believeth in him should not perish, but have everlasting life."

The obelisk on the Thames embankment in London today.

each. The plaque on the land side of the pedestal reads, "This obelisk, prostrate for centuries in the sands of Alexandria, was presented to the British nation A.D. 1819, by Mohammed Ali, Viceroy of Egypt,—a worthy memorial of our distinguished countrymen, Nelson and Abercromby." Another plaque honored John Dixon and Erasmus Wilson.

The ceremony was curiously low-key, with no official festivities. Although General Alexander and Erasmus Wilson had hoped for royal and governmental participation, they were informed at the last minute, without explanation, that there would be none. The reason for the government keeping its distance was probably connected with the increasing British influence in Egypt that would result in 1882 with the establishment of an informal protectorate. The government probably thought that publically embracing a gift of the khedive in London would make it harder to undermine his authority in Egypt.

While there have been occasional murmurs about returning Cleopatra's Needle to Egypt, it remains on the Thames Embankment and, like the Elgin Marbles in the British Museum, is unlikely to be repatriated.

.

CHAPTER SIX

Reaching the Top

WITH THE END of the Civil War, the stump of the Washington Monument became more and more of an embarrassment to the city and the nation. On Washington's birthday in 1866, President Andrew Johnson addressed the Washington National Monument Society, of which he was ex-officio president. "Let us restore the Union," he said, "and let us proceed with the Monument as its symbol until it shall contain the pledge of all the States of the Union. . . . Let your monument rise . . . higher and higher until it shall meet the sun in his coming, and his last parting ray shall linger and play on its summit."

The estimated cost of completing the monument was seven hundred thousand dollars, and the society had on hand only $1,281.06. Congress was asked every year for help, but, while it offered encouragement, it failed to provide any money, claiming that the enormous debt run up by the Civil War made that impossible.* One bill submitted in 1869 called for forming a "Washington Monument Union" with such members as A. T. Stewart and Cornelius Vanderbilt, presumably as a vehicle for those two and others to underwrite the monument's completion.† They didn't bite.

In 1871, the society again appealed to the public. The limit on contributions of one dollar a year was now a distant memory, and the society promised to chisel the names of contributors of five thousand dollars or more onto a block to be installed in the monument. Those contributing one thousand dollars or more would have their names recorded on a tablet. Those contributing one hundred dollars or more would have their names inscribed on a list to be kept in the society's archives.

The State of New York appropriated ten thousand dollars for the monument's completion, but the money was only to be paid when there was enough money on hand for work to begin again. Other states made similar pledges. But

---

* The national debt rose from $64 million in 1860 to $2.755 billion in 1866. In 1865, the federal government became the first government in world history to spend more than $1 billion in a single year.

† A. T. Stewart (1803–76) had more or less invented the department store and was one of the country's largest importers of luxury dry goods. His wealth was probably second only to that of Cornelius Vanderbilt (1794–1877), whose railroad empire was growing rapidly at this point. He had taken control of the New York Central in 1867 and would acquire the Lake Shore and Southern Michigan railroad in 1869, connecting him to Chicago.

little actual money flowed into the coffers of the society. In 1871 it collected a paltry $1,008 in donations and accrued interest.

Part of the problem was that not everybody liked the design. To be sure, a select committee of Congress had written that "this rich and massive shaft, though simple and plain, would be a noble monument, worthy of the sublime character which it is designed to testify." Senator Thomas F. Bayard of Delaware, however, called it a "blot upon architecture." Mark Twain thought it looked like "a factory chimney with the top broken off." Even its original architect, Robert Mills, thought that without the elaborate surrounding pantheon he had designed, the obelisk, when completed, would look like a "stalk of asparagus."

The 1870s were the height of Victorian architectural exuberance, a time when more was more. What is now the Eisenhower Executive Office Building, built between 1871 and 1888 just west of the White House to house the departments of war, state, and the navy, was the epitome of architectural fashion, with its mansard roof and rich architectural ornamentation in the lush Second Empire style.*

---

* As architectural fashion changed, the Eisenhower Executive Office Building came to be regarded as one of the ugliest in Washington. Harry Truman called it "the greatest monstrosity in America" and it was nearly torn down in 1957. But by 1969 fashions were again changing and it was designated a national historic landmark, making it safe from the wrecker's ball. The office suites originally designed for the secretaries of war, state, and the navy (which is now the vice president's official office) have been restored in all their Victorian grandeur. It is a perfect example of the dictum that "Every generation thinks that its art is art; that its parents' art is ugly, that its grandparents' art is quaint; and its great grandparents' art is art."

The Washington Monument would have no architectural ornamentation whatever, despite numerous plans and proposals to add some in the Gothic or Renaissance style. One plan sought to merge "modern French Renaissance" style with "some of the better Hindu pagodas."*

Another concern was whether the foundation as originally planned and built was adequate to support the 91,000-ton weight of the completed structure. In 1874, a report from Lieutenant W. L. Marshall of the Army Corps of Engineers stated that "it seems inadvisable to complete the Washington Monument to the full height of 600 feet. The area covered by the foundation is too small for a structure of the proposed dimensions and weight, causing an excess pressure upon a soil not wholly incompressible."

There were two solutions: reinforce the foundations or lower the final height so as to lessen the ultimate weight. Marshall recommended a height of no more than 437 feet and the upper part to be built of lighter materials, such as brick. He also recommended eliminating Mills's pantheon, which was probably the final nail in its coffin.

---

* Any major building, it seems, produces critics if it is out of the ordinary, as all great buildings are. Many French intellectuals and artists, such as the short-story writer Guy de Maupassant and the composers Charles Gounod and Jules Massenet, fought the erection of the Eiffel Tower between 1885 and 1889. A "Committee of Three Hundred"—one for each meter of the tower's proposed height—was formed to protest it, writing, "We, writers, painters, sculptors, architects and passionate devotees of the hitherto untouched beauty of Paris, protest with all our strength, with all our indignation in the name of slighted French taste, against the erection . . . of this useless and monstrous Eiffel Tower." After it was built, Maupassant was said to have lunched in the tower restaurant every day as it was the only place in Paris where he didn't have to look at it. Today, of course, Paris without the Eiffel Tower is almost inconceivable.

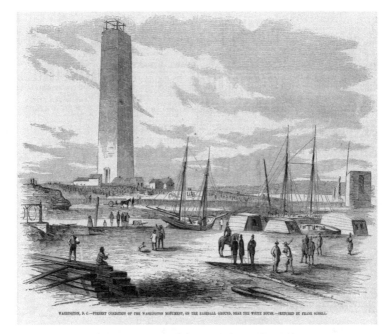

The Washington Monument under construction circa 1874.

Finally, on July 5, 1876, the day after the nation's centennial, Senator John Sherman of Ohio offered a joint resolution that the Senate and House of Representatives, "in the name of the people of the United States, at the beginning of the second century of the national existence, do assume and direct the completion of the Washington Monument, in the City of Washington." It was unanimously adopted by both houses.*

---

* John Sherman was a major Republican figure in the second half of the nineteenth century, serving as secretary of the treasury and of state as well as senator. He was a contender for the Republican presidential nomination three times and the principal author of the Sherman Antitrust Act. His older brother was General William

The final bill appropriated two hundred thousand dollars for the monument's completion, required that the foundation issue be definitively settled before construction could renew, and stipulated that the Washington National Monument Society convey title to "all property, rights, and privileges belonging to it in the Monument." The bill also established a Joint Commission on the Construction of the Washington National Monument. The members were the president of the United States, the architect of the Treasury Department, the architect of the Capitol, the chief of engineers of the Army Corps of Engineers, and the first vice president of the society.

President Ulysses S. Grant signed the bill into law on August 2, 1876.

The society put out one more appeal for funds but apparently people felt that now that Congress had appropriated funds, it would have no choice but to continue to do so until the monument was finished, and little money came in.

THE FOUNDATIONS WERE examined once again and found wanting to support the full weight. Though they were twenty-four feet thick, with eight feet above ground, they were constructed in part of rubble only partly held together with cement. At a depth of thirteen feet there was

---

Tecumseh Sherman. Senator Sherman added the phrase "fence mending" to the country's political vocabulary.

water and below that was a bed of a mixture of clay and fine sand, the exact ratio of clay and sand varying both by depth and at each of the corners. Because the mixture varied, parts of it were more compressible than other parts, causing a concern that the obelisk would lean. Even at a mere 178 feet high, the monument was leaning slightly toward the north and west and exhibiting an "increasing departure from horizontality." The engineers warned against a load of more than five tons per square foot. The full weight of the completed monument would exert a force of eleven tons per square foot.

A joint resolution of Congress authorized that the foundations be strengthened and appropriated thirty-six thousand dollars for the job. General Andrew Humphreys, the Chief of Engineers, put Lieutenant Colonel Thomas Lincoln Casey in charge of both fixing the foundation and completing the monument.

Thomas Casey came from a distinguished military family. His father, Silas Casey, a major general in the Civil War, had led the assault on Chapultepec Castle at the climax of the Mexican-American War. Graduating first in his class at West Point in 1852, Casey was assigned to the Corps of Engineers and taught engineering at West Point until 1859. A gifted and no-nonsense administrator, Casey, after the Civil War, was assigned to the office of the chief of engineers and oversaw numerous projects in Washington, including the building of the Eisenhower Executive Office Building.

He ordered still another study of the foundation and, concluding that it would not do, hired miners, who were

THOMAS LINCOLN CASEY
1857-1925

Lt. Col. Thomas Lincoln Casey, who oversaw the completion of the Washington Monument.

used to working underground and willing to tolerate the dangers of tunneling under the foundations of so vast a structure. Pairs of tunnels were constructed from opposite sides to assure an even strain, reaching down fourteen feet beneath the old foundation. Seventy percent of the earth beneath the foundation was removed and the void filled with a massive concrete footing that reached out thirty-five feet from the old foundation. When the miners were finished, the old foundation had been encased in a concrete pyramid one hundred feet square at its base. The new foundation was two and a half times the size of the old one and reached more than thirteen feet deeper.

Strengthening the foundation of the Washington Monument, early 1880s.

Some critics still wanted to add ornamentation to the monument but Casey, wise in the ways of Washington in general and Congress in particular (he had advised on how to improve the ventilation of the House chamber among his many projects), swatted them away, playing on Congressional interest in no more delays.

Casey was planning to build the monument to a height of six hundred feet. But the United States Minister to Italy, George Perkins Marsh, wrote George F. Edmunds, senator from Vermont, asking whether the rising monument would conform to the proportions of the ancient Egyptian obelisks. Edmunds passed the letter on to Casey.

George Perkins Marsh was one of the more remarkable of the polymaths with which the nineteenth century so abounded. Born in Vermont of a distinguished family (his father served as a congressman), he attended Andover and Dartmouth, graduating with highest honors, and then studied law. He served in Congress in the 1840s and in 1849 President Zachary Taylor appointed him as minister to the Ottoman Empire. In 1861, when the Kingdom of Italy was proclaimed, President Lincoln named him minister (ambassador), a post he would hold for twenty-one years until his death, longer than any other American diplomat has served as chief of mission.

Aside from his public career, he was a scholar of languages, fluent in twenty, including Icelandic, his specialty. He was also a keen student of nature. He wrote such varied books as *A Compendious Grammar of the Old-Northern or Icelandic Language* and *The Camel, his Organization, Habits, and Uses, with Reference to his Introduction into the United States*. His masterpiece was *Man and Nature*, later rewritten as *The Earth as Modified by Human Action*, one of the earliest works on the aborning science of ecology; he is considered the father of the science of human ecology.

Marsh had studied the eleven Egyptian obelisks that stand in Rome and found that they had a base-to-height ratio of ten to one. Since the base of the Washington

Monument was fixed at 55 feet 1½ inches, if following the ancient formula was important, then its proper height should be 551 feet 3 inches.* Marsh also advised on the proportions of the pyramidion, saying that it should slope at an angle of seventy-three degrees from the horizontal. He urged that Mills's pantheon be scrapped and that there be no ornamentation whatever. Casey agreed with him fully.

Casey had originally thought to construct the pyramidion of glass and iron, a new construction technique that had been pioneered in the great Crystal Palace at the first world's fair in London in 1851. Marsh vehemently disagreed, saying that it would look absurd. "The obelisk is not an arbitrary structure," he wrote Casey. ". . . Its objects, forms and proportions were fixed by the usage of thousands of years; they satisfy every cultivated eye, and I hold it an esthetical crime to depart from them." Marsh, at least, conceded that windows at the top would be inevitable.

Casey tore down the twenty-eight feet of substandard marble and granite that had been erected by the Know-Nothings and ordered that the new marble "must be white, strong, sound . . . and must in texture and color so conform to the marble now built in the monument as not to present any marked or striking contrast in color luster or shade."†

---

* The final height was long thought to be 555 feet, five and a half inches. But the *New York Times* reported in 1999 that scientists, using satellites to get the most accurate measurement yet, determined that the monument was actually 555 feet, five and nine-tenths inch tall.

† In this he did not get his way and the contrast between the first 150 feet and the rest of the monument is striking. It's a standard Washington joke that the line marks the high-water mark of a Potomac River flood.

Four columns, each a little less than six inches in diameter and made of wrought iron about four tenths of an inch thick, provided the framework for the stairs. At this point it also, more importantly, provided the framework for the steam-powered hoist that lifted the marble and granite blocks to the working level. When completed, the hoist machinery would be converted into the elevator machinery for lifting people to the top. It thus had to precede the building of the walls.

Finally, the Washington Monument was ready to renew its climb to the sky. On August 7, 1880, Colonel Casey, President Rutherford B. Hayes, and several other dignitaries were lifted by the hoist to the 150-foot level. Hayes marked a coin with his initials and the date and placed it beneath the new cornerstone that marked the renewed construction.

The monument began its now steady climb. It reached 176 feet by the end of that year. By the end of 1881 it stood at 250 feet, not yet half way. And a year later it had reached the 340-foot mark.

ON NOVEMBER 12, 1884, the monument reached the height of 520 feet and thus became the tallest structure in the world, topping the spires of Cologne Cathedral, which rise 515 feet above the ground. As the monument finally approached completion that fall, the question of what to top it off with had to be decided. Casey had originally intended to have it finished with the same marble used for the facing. But, as the monument would be the tallest point for many miles around (until the completion of the Eiffel Tower in 1889, it remained the tallest structure in the world), it would need a lightning rod.

Casey intended to have a copper rod, topped with silver, protrude from the peak, which would connect with the four interior columns that held the stairs and elevator, guiding the car up and down the shaft. These hollow columns stood on cast-iron shoes set in a pit below the monument's floor. Soft copper rods led from there to the earth.

But soon, Casey, perhaps inspired by the ancient Egyptian practice of covering the pyramidion with gold or electrum to catch the first rays of the morning sun, thought about the apex of the monument being cast in solid metal to function as the tip of the lightning rod system.

He worried about the metal deteriorating and perhaps staining the marble beneath it, so he wrote to a Philadelphia metallurgist named William Frishmuth asking him the cost of casting a small pyramid about five inches square at the base and rising about nine inches, to be placed at the apex of the pyramidion.* To ensure that it would not stain the marble, he wanted it plated in platinum, the least reactive of all metals, and thought the pyramid itself might be of copper, bronze, or brass.

---

* Casey was notoriously frugal and fastidious with the Treasury's money. He had even written that fall asking permission to serve hot coffee to the workers high atop the monument—coffee cost about ten cents a pound in the 1880s—to help them stay warm as winter approached. The Treasury allowed the expense.

Frishmuth replied, via a collect telegram, suggesting that the metal used be aluminum, a metal then very rare in its pure form.

Aluminum is the most abundant metallic element in the earth's crust, making up 8.3 percent by weight. Of all the elements, only oxygen and silicon are more abundant. Aluminum is shiny with a high reflectivity (which is why it is used to coat the mirrors of reflecting telescopes). It is ductile, malleable, nonmagnetic, and very light. It does not tarnish. Pure aluminum, reacting with air, quickly develops a skin of transparent aluminum oxide only four nanometers thick, which stops any further oxidation.*

Despite its ubiquity, aluminum was not even suspected to exist until the late eighteenth century because, highly reactive, it rarely occurs in a pure state. The ancient Greeks and Romans knew about aluminum salts, which they used in dyeing and as an astringent, but had no understanding of their chemistry.†

In 1808 the great British chemist Sir Humphry Davy identified that the base of the aluminum salt called alum was a metal and coined the word *aluminum* (or in British English, *aluminium*). In 1827 the German chemist Friedrich Wöhler discovered how to purify aluminum by a complex chemical process that involved potassium. But

---

* Naturally occurring crystals of aluminum oxide are known as corundum. Add a little chromium to aluminum oxide and you have a ruby. Other impurities produce sapphires.

† Aluminum salts are still used today in such things as styptic pencils, which stanch bleeding because the salts cause tissue to contract.

pure aluminum was exceedingly expensive to produce by this process, initially costing more than gold.*

By the 1880s the price of aluminum had dropped to about the price of silver, roughly a dollar an ounce, thanks to an improved—but still complicated and difficult—chemical process for extracting it that used expensive sodium rather than the very expensive potassium.

But aluminum production was still tiny. While world silver production in 1884 was some 2,627 tons, aluminum production was only four tons. Clemens Winckler, a leader in the metal industry, explained in *Scientific American* in 1879 that "there are several reasons why the metal is shown so little favor . . . First of all there is the price; then the methods of working it are not everywhere known; and further, no one knows how to cast it." In other words, aluminum had a chicken-and-egg problem. The price was high because the technology was primitive, but there had been little technical advancement because the price was so high.

William Frishmuth was the only foundry owner in the country producing and utilizing pure aluminum. In 1884 he produced about 112 pounds of aluminum 97.75 percent pure. The peak of the Washington Monument would be the largest aluminum casting ever made up to that point and Frishmuth assured Casey that if casting so large a piece of aluminum proved impossible, he would make it from

---

* In the 1850s Emperor Napoleon III is supposed to have given a dinner at which the most important guests were given aluminum flatware while the other guests had to make do with gold.

aluminum bronze, an alloy of 90 percent copper and 10 percent aluminum that was made from aluminum oxide and widely known. He said that if he made the piece from aluminum he would charge seventy-five dollars. If he made it from bronze, he would charge fifty dollars for the finished piece plated in gold and seventy-five dollars if plated in platinum.

Although ever the penny-pincher, Casey realized that they were on the technological cutting edge and wrote Frishmuth that "it is desired that the cost be kept, if possible, within the estimate which you submitted, but should that cost be necessarily and unavoidably exceeded in producing a perfect piece of workmanship, the account shall be submitted setting forth that fact."

Frishmuth quickly found out that an ordinary sand casting would not be possible and ordered an iron mold. Within two weeks, however, on November 12, he was able to telegraph Casey that he had succeeded. "After hard work and disappointments, I have just cast a perfect pyramide of pure aluminum made of South Carolina Corundum. Great honor to you, the Monument and whole people of North America & a little to myself lent. Cost of pyramide more than calculated. However will state the facts."

Frishmuth submitted a bill for $256.10, more than three times his original estimate, and Casey immediately sent his assistant to Philadelphia to investigate. They eventually settled on a payment of $225. Frishmuth wanted some publicity for his accomplishment and put the apex on display in Philadelphia and then at Tiffany's in New York.

People who came to see it were allowed to step over it and thus be able to claim, honestly after a fashion, that they had once stepped over the top of the Washington Monument.*

Casey received the casting on November 29, and he wrote Frishmuth to say that "the point is received and is acceptable in every way."

On one side of the apex were engraved the names of the engineers and mechanics who had overseen the final phase of construction. On another side was inscribed, "Cornerstone laid on bed of foundation July 4, 1848. First stone at height of 152 feet, laid August 7, 1880. Capstone set Dec. 6, 1884." A third side read, "Joint Commission at setting of capstone—Chester A. Arthur; W. W. Corcoran, Chairman; M. E. Bell, Edward Clark, John Newton. Act of Aug. 2, 1876." The fourth side said simply, "Laus Deo" (Latin for "Praise God").

On December 6, 1884, it was set in place. A little after two in the afternoon, Casey, his assistants, and several workmen stood on a narrow platform and set the capstone, which weighed 6,300 pounds. "The capstone was set by

---

* Because of the apex of the Washington Monument, many people heard of the semi-precious metal aluminum for the first time. Ironically, less than two years later, the Hall-Héroult process to smelt aluminum was independently developed by Charles Martin Hall in the United States and Paul Héroult in France. Using electricity in very large amounts, the process drastically reduced the cost of the purified metal and thus greatly expanded its potential uses.

Because of the amount of electricity required to turn aluminum ore, such as bauxite, into aluminum, aluminum smelters are usually located in places, however far from the bauxite mines, where hydroelectric power is abundant, such as Arvida, Quebec, 150 miles north of Quebec City.

By the mid-twentieth century, aluminum was being used extensively in airplane manufacture and for such mundane quotidian tasks as wrapping leftovers.

The pinnacle of the Washington Monument, made of aluminum.

me," Casey later wrote, "and the Aluminum point secured
. . . thus substantially completing the walls of the obelisk."
The capstone had been cut to make room for the aluminum
point and the latter simply screwed in to the copper rod
coming up through a hole in the capstone.

Dignitaries had been invited to the modest ceremony
and most of them stood on a platform at the five-hundred-
foot level or remained inside the monument. As the *New
York Times* explained, "A steady downpour of rain had given

place a little while previously to a brisk gale of wind at this elevation (blowing about 55 miles an hour), and very few of the invited guests cared to avail themselves of the privilege of climbing the nearly perpendicular ladder from the 500-foot platform to the dizzy height of 533 feet, from which three or four journalists and a half dozen adventurous climbers witnessed the setting of the capstone and subsequently ascended to the pinnacle."

With the capstone and aluminum pinnacle in place, an American flag was hoisted above the monument to the height of exactly six hundred feet. As the flag was raised, an artillery battery on the White House grounds, a few hundred yards away, fired a twenty-one-gun salute, and faint cheering from the crowd on the ground below could be heard.

Dedication of the Washington Monument, December 6, 1884.

Not everyone was impressed. The next day, the *New York Times* sniffed that "at least it is a satisfaction to know that the scheme which has been dragging for nearly forty years is now out of the way, even if the result be a monument undesigned, ill placed, and at one stage of its construction ill built. Perhaps the next Washington monument that we feel moved to erect may be something not absurdly unworthy of its subject. In the meantime we have the sweet consciousness that the Washington Monument is the tallest structure in the world."

BECAUSE FEBRUARY 22, 1885—George Washington's one hundred fifty-third birthday—was a Sunday, the dedication ceremony took place the day before, a cold, windy day with snow on the ground. The ceremony began with Senator John Sherman, the chairman of the joint Congressional committee, who declared before an audience of about eight hundred people that "the Monument speaks for itself—simple in form, admirable in proportion, composed of enduring marble and granite, resting upon foundations broad and deep, it rises into the skies higher than any other work of human art. It is the most imposing, costly and appropriate monument ever erected to the memory of one man."

Then came a prayer, band music, and an address by the elderly W. W. Corcoran of the Washington National Monument Society, read by the president of Columbia University. The *New York Times* reporter on hand noted that "the remarks of the various speakers were inaudible, but the puffs of steam from their mouths was evidence that the proceedings were being carried on according to the progamme and at every little intermission the spectators stamped approvingly."

Robert Winthrop, the speaker of the House who had spoken at the dedication of the cornerstone almost thirty-seven years earlier, was too feeble to speak himself, but he wrote a speech that was read out for him by Representative John D. Long, a notably good public speaker.

Then it was the turn of the Masons, using the same ceremony that George Washington had participated in at the laying of the Capitol cornerstone in 1793. Grand Master Myron M. Parker asked his deputy the uses of the square, and the deputy replied, "To square our actions by the square of virtue, and prove our work when finished."

"Have you applied the square to the Obelisk, and is the work squared?"

"I have, and I find the corners to be square; the workmen have done their duty."*

Finally, Colonel Casey formally presented the monument to the nation on behalf of the joint commission for its completion.

President Chester A. Arthur, who had earlier reviewed an honor guard commanded by General Philip Sheridan of

---

* The Masons are, famously, supposed to keep their rituals and words secret. But they are nearly all to be easily found in books and, nowadays, on the Internet. Benjamin Franklin, a Mason, as were many of the Founding Fathers, once joked that the only thing secret about the Masons was the fact that they had no secrets.

Civil War fame while wearing a fur-lined overcoat because of the weather, spoke in the flowery oratory so beloved of the Victorians of the man being honored. He described Washington as possessing "the faith that never faltered, the wisdom that was broader and deeper than any learning taught in schools, the courage that shrank from no peril and was dismayed by no defeat, the loyalty that kept all selfish purpose subordinate to the demands of patriotism and honor, the sagacity that displayed itself in camp and cabinet alike, and above all that harmonious union of moral and intellectual qualities which has never found its parallel among men."

Finally he got around to actually accepting the monument. "I do now, as President of the United States and in behalf of the people, receive this monument from the hands of its builders and declare it dedicated from this time forth to the immortal name and memory of George Washington."

Fireworks that evening included one that depicted a ghostly George Washington on horseback.

After more than eighty years of proposals, plans, fundraising drives, Congressional dithering, and building, the construction of Washington's monument was finally finished.

CHAPTER SEVEN

Securing New York's
Moral Grandeur

WITH THE OPENING of the Erie Canal in 1825, New York City had begun to grow explosively. The rapidly expanding trans-Appalachian commerce that had once, out of necessity, flowed down the Mississippi and through the port of New Orleans could now begin to flow instead through the Great Lakes, the canal, and then down the Hudson River to the port of New York.

The city's development began to roar uptown at the rate of two blocks a year.* It was the greatest boomtown in

---

*That might not seem like much, but Manhattan Island is about two miles wide. That meant that the city was adding about ten miles of developed street front per year, a pace that continued for decades.

human history. But, like most boomtowns, it was a raw place, ugly, badly governed, and—except for the New-York Historical Society, founded in 1804—lacking in cultural amenities such as museums, monuments, and opera houses. The novelist Edith Wharton (1862–1937) remembered the city of her childhood as "this little, low-studded, rectangular New York, cursed with its universal chocolate-colored coating of the most hideous stone ever quarried."

The city's rawness began to fade after the Civil War, which had contributed greatly to New York's swiftly growing wealth. Its leading citizens began to organize to provide the amenities that would help New York join the ranks of the world's great cities as a center of culture as well as commerce and finance. The American Museum of Natural History was founded in 1869, the Metropolitan Museum of Art in 1870, the Metropolitan Opera in 1880, Carnegie Hall in 1891. The New York Public Library, now the fourth largest library in the world, was founded in 1895. By the turn of the century, New York was rapidly becoming the equal of Paris and London as a world cultural center.

And among its new cultural icons, as with those two cities, was an ancient Egyptian obelisk. It was, and remains to this day, the only one in the western hemisphere.

WHILE FRANCE AND Great Britain acquired title to their obelisks in the early nineteenth century, when the Egyptian government and people cared little if anything for the country's vast trove of antiquities, by the latter half of the nineteenth century that attitude was beginning to change. Fortunately for New York, the khedive of Egypt, Ismail Pasha (ruled 1863–79), was determined to modernize Egypt, whatever the expense, and had run up ruinous debts, as much as one hundred million pounds. In 1875 he had been forced to sell Egypt's shares in the Suez Canal to the British government, giving Britain control of Egypt's greatest strategic asset. He wanted to increase Egyptian-American trade to help relieve the fiscal straits he was still in, and he was also anxious to increase Egyptian-American friendship in hopes of fending off increasing European interference in Egyptian affairs.

In 1869, at the opening of the Suez Canal, the khedive had first suggested to William Henry Hurlbert, the editor of the New York *World*, the idea of Egypt giving an ancient obelisk to the United States as a token of friendship.

Another nineteenth-century polymath, Hurlbert was raised in both the North and the South and would always feel sympathy for both sides. He earned a B.A. from Harvard and, two years later, a divinity degree and became an ordained Unitarian minister, although he practiced that profession only briefly. Fluent in several languages, he toured Europe, where he was often taken for a native, regardless of what country he was in.

In the 1850s he wrote a successful play and then became the lead editorial writer for the *New York Times*. He would be a journalist for most of the rest of his life, noted for his fluid prose style and easy grasp of whatever matter he was writing about.

But Hurlbert is today most famous for a book he never acknowledged having written at all. Indeed, the authorship of *The Diary of a Public Man* was one of the great mysteries of American historiography from the time it was first published in the *North American Review* in 1879 until 2010, when historian Daniel W. Croft, using both literary analysis and the statistical analysis known as stylometry, made a convincing case that Hurlbert was the author.

The Diary of a Public Man, which is really a memoir, deals with the period from December 28, 1860, to March 15, 1861, as the union was falling apart. It has verbatim conversations between the author and such Washington insiders

William Henry Hurlbert, editor of the New York *World*, campaigned to bring an obelisk to New York.

as Stephen A. Douglas, William H. Seward, and Abraham Lincoln, offering remarkable insights into their thinking and actions as they tried to prevent civil war and save the union. American historians have long accepted the work as a genuine and invaluable historical source.

Hurlbert tried to interest such New York social and financial leaders as William Henry Vanderbilt (eldest son of Cornelius Vanderbilt) and Henry G. Stebbins in the project of getting an Egyptian obelisk for New York. At first there was little support for the idea. But when London's obelisk was erected on the Thames Embankment in 1878, it caused a sudden and intense outbreak of obelisk fever in New York.

In 1881, the *New York Herald*, more than a little tongue in cheek, observed that "it would be absurd for the people of any great city to hope to be happy without an Egyptian obelisk. Rome has had them this great while and so has Constantinople. Paris has one. London has one. If New York was without one, all those great sites might point the finger of scorn at us and intimate that we could never rise to any real moral grandeur until we had our obelisk."

Vanderbilt and Stebbins now moved to secure the prize and ensure their city's "moral grandeur."

Cornelius Vanderbilt, known as the Commodore, had died in 1877, the richest self-made man in the world. He left most of his fortune of $105 million to his son William Henry, who, a highly capable businessman himself, would double the family fortune in the next eight years. Shortly before his death, he told a friend that he was worth

$194 million and would not cross the street to make another million. He didn't have to as his income, as reckoned by *Harper's Weekly*, was about one million dollars a month at a time when one thousand dollars a year was a decent income.

It is a measure of just how large Vanderbilt loomed in the American consciousness in the 1880s that the day after he died suddenly in December 1885, the front page of the *New York Times* carried no other news whatever.

Henry G. Stebbins, while nowhere near as rich as Vanderbilt, moved in the same social circles. A Wall Street broker, he had served three times as president of the New York Stock Exchange and one term as a Congressman. He

Henry G. Stebbins.

had been commodore of the New York Yacht Club and was a founding trustee of both the Metropolitan Museum of Art and the American Museum of Natural History.

As president of the Board of Commissioners of Central Park, which guided the creation of the park between 1857 and 1870, Stebbins had been instrumental in awarding the commission for the famous *Angel of the Waters* statue at Bethesda Fountain in the heart of the park. It was the first major commission in New York awarded to a female artist. The fact that the artist in question was Emma Stebbins, Henry's sister, earned him considerable criticism in the newspapers. Regardless of the flagrant nepotism, the *Angel of the Waters* is today, after the Statue of Liberty, perhaps the city's most iconic statue.

To make sure that the khedive's offer to Hurlbert was still good, Stebbins asked the secretary of state, William M. Evarts, to use diplomatic pressure and Evarts instructed Elbert Farman, the American consul general in Egypt, to exert it.*

Farman asked for an interview with the khedive, who told him that while he would, personally, be happy to give New York an obelisk there was a political problem. The obelisk in question was the mate to the one recently erected in London. Unlike its twin, it had not fallen but still stood erect on the shoreline of Alexandria, and he feared the reaction of the people of that city.

---

*The American power elite was a small world in those days. Evarts was, while serving as secretary of state, also president of the Union Club, New York's oldest club, of which both Stebbins and Vanderbilt were members.

While the Egyptian population as a whole, wretchedly poor for the most part, was still largely unaware of or at least indifferent to the country's ancient patrimony, the population of Alexandria was a different matter. Since its founding by Alexander the Great in 331 B.C., the city had always been an international crossroads with a large and diverse foreign population. Long-staple cotton had been introduced to Egypt in 1820 and soon became a major cash crop that was brokered through Alexandria with European cloth manufacturers, and this foreign population of traders and financiers objected to giving away the obelisk.

Farman kept up gentle pressure on the khedive over the next year. Finally, at a dinner party one night, the khedive invited him to talk. When they had settled themselves, the khedive said, "Well, Mr. Farman, you would like an obelisk."

Farman noted at the time, "turns of the wheel of fortune are not only frequent in Egypt, but they generally happen when least expected." He feared that the khedive would not long remain in power and so he asked for a confirmation of the gift in writing.* On May 18, 1879, he received the letter, which read,

> The Government of the Khedive having taken into
> consideration your representations, and the desire which
> you have expressed in the name of the Government of the

---

* Farman was correct. The khedive was forced to abdicate in favor of his son a month later. In 1882, British and French forces bombarded the city to force Egypt to pay its debts to them and Egypt soon became, at least de facto, a British protectorate.

"Cleopatra's Needle" by the harbor in Alexandria, Egypt, before its removal to New York.

United States of America, consent, in fact to make a gift to the city of New York of the obelisk known as Cleopatra's Needle, which is at Alexandria on the sea-shore.

The pair of obelisks had been known as Cleopatra's Needles since the Middle Ages though they had nothing whatever to do with Egypt's last pharaoh. Indeed they were already 1,400 years old when Cleopatra VII came to the throne, having been ordered by Thutmose III, who reigned from c.1479 to c.1425 B.C. Under the thumb of his stepmother, the pharaoh Hatshepsut, until she died in 1458 B.C., Thutmose, once reigning in his own right, soon proved himself one of the most energetic and successful rulers of ancient Egypt. He conquered provinces as far north as Syria and as far south as Nubia.

Like all successful and long-reigning pharaohs, Thutmose built lavishly, including at least three pairs of obelisks. One pair was placed outside the temple of Luxor, where one remains upright (the other graces the Place de la Concorde). Another pair was placed outside the Temple of the Sun in Heliopolis.*

There the pair stayed for nine hundred years, undisturbed except that Rameses II (reigned 1279–1212 B.C.) added hieroglyphic inscriptions to his own glory, as he did to so many ancient Egyptian monuments. In 920 B.C. the far more obscure pharaoh Osorkon added his own name to each of the obelisks. Then in 525 B.C., the Persian Empire invaded Egypt and burned Heliopolis. Both obelisks fell in the chaos and lay on their sides for another five hundred years.

Egypt became a province of the Roman Empire in 30 B.C. and about 10 B.C., after Augustus ordered the two obelisks floated down the Nile to Alexandria, they were erected in front of the Caesareum, the temple honoring the deified Julius Caesar, Augustus's adoptive father. Because the corners at the bottom of the obelisks had broken off,

---

* That, of course, is the Greek name, meaning City of the Sun. The Egyptian name for the city was On.

the Romans installed a bronze support in the shape of a crab on each to stabilize it.

Although the shifting seashore caused the destruction of much of the Caesareum, the obelisks endured until the early fourteenth century when a massive earthquake toppled the one that was ultimately given to Great Britain. This may have been the same earthquake that completed the destruction of the Pharos, Alexandria's great lighthouse. It had been one of the seven wonders of the ancient world and had signaled the entrance to Alexandria's harbor since early in the third century B.C.

With title to the obelisk secured, William H. Vanderbilt soon agreed to fund the whole moving operation, just as Erasmus Wilson had paid to move the London obelisk. But Vanderbilt's generosity was alloyed with a bit of embarrassment. Stebbins and other members of the Central Park Commission wanted to start a subscription fund to pay for the move. To get the fund off to a good start, they called on Vanderbilt and asked him to make the first contribution. A cautious man who liked to think things through, Vanderbilt told them he wanted to look at the options and that they should come back to his office the following Tuesday for an answer.

They did so, only to learn that Vanderbilt, having apparently forgotten about the appointment, had left for Buffalo the previous day. Stebbins telegraphed Vanderbilt in Buffalo to say that they had kept the appointment only to find Vanderbilt not there. A few hours later they received a telegram back from an embarrassed Vanderbilt saying,

William Henry Vanderbilt.

"Arrange to bring the obelisk at once [to] Central [Park]. I will pay the entire expense."

With the money now in hand, a plan was needed to lower the obelisk to the ground, transport it to a ship, load it and sail it across the Mediterranean Sea and Atlantic Ocean, unload it from the ship in New York, transport the obelisk to a landing site in Manhattan, transport it through the streets of the city to the designated spot in Central Park, and erect it for the third and hopefully last time in its long existence.

Even in the late nineteenth century that was no mean feat of engineering. Cleopatra's Needle stands sixty-nine feet high and nearly eight feet on a side at the base. It weighs about two hundred and twenty tons and its base weighs another fifty tons.

Four plans were submitted for consideration, but three of them were incomplete and, indeed, fanciful. One called for the obelisk to be slung under a ship's keel on chains. Another was to encase the obelisk in enough wood that it would float and then tow it across the Atlantic.

The plan that was approved had been carefully thought out by a naval engineer named Henry Honychurch Gorringe. Born in Barbados in 1841, the son of the rector of Saint Michael's Cathedral, Gorringe went to sea in the American merchant marine as a teenager. In 1862 he enlisted in the navy and after the Civil War he decided to stay in the navy and received a regular commission. In 1868 he was promoted to lieutenant commander.

Gorringe was active in mapping the sea floor of the Atlantic and in 1875, in command of the sidewheeler USS *Gettysburg*, he discovered what is now known as the Gorringe Sea Bank east of the Azores. Between 1876 and 1878 Gorringe prepared hydrographic charts of the Mediterranean and became familiar with the obelisk. He thought deeply about how to move it to New York. His detailed plan was accepted, as was his request for seventy-five thousand dollars to fund the project. What was left over would be his fee.* Gorringe asked for a leave of absence

---

*That was an enormous sum in the late nineteenth century when five thousand dollars a year was a very comfortable upper-middle-class income. But it was only about 7.5 percent of William H. Vanderbilt's monthly income.

Naval engineer Henry Honeychurch Gorringe.

from the navy and convinced fellow naval officer Lieutenant Seaton Schroeder to be his assistant. Schroeder
readily agreed. As Schroeder wrote, Gorringe "suddenly
appeared in Washington and took me out for a private talk,
the subject of which was the removal of the obelisk, and he
asked if I would go with him. That was a call that I could
not resist."

Gorringe had studied earlier obelisk transportation
methods, including those of ancient times. As an experi-
enced seaman, he realized that the most difficult part of the
whole transportation and reerection problem would be

getting the obelisk onto and off of a vessel. In his book on the saga of moving the obelisk, he wrote

> that the vessel in which the New York obelisk was to be transported must be large enough to take care of herself under all conditions of weather, and must have her own motive power [a reference to the near disaster with moving the London obelisk]. . . . [As for the obelisk] its size was as embarrassing as its weight. No vessel has hatches that will admit a mass sixty-nine feet in length. It could not have been carried on deck in safety without strengthening the vessel at great expense. In the hold, below the waterline, was the only place where it could be securely stowed and safely transported, and how to get it there was the one thing on which the whole operation of removing it successfully turned.
>
> The plan devised and successfully executed consisted simply in embarking and disembarking the obelisk while the bow of the vessel was out of water, through an aperture opened expressly for the purpose and subsequently closed for the voyage.

Gorringe designed a structure for turning the obelisk from vertical to horizontal. It was built by the firm of John A. Roebling's Sons in Trenton, New Jersey, then also busily engaged in building the Brooklyn Bridge, which opened in 1883. The structure was designed to be transported in pieces to Alexandria where it would be reassembled. Afterward it was to be disassembled again and returned to New York in the same ship as the obelisk itself and used to erect the obelisk in Central Park.

Gorringe and Schroeder arrived in Alexandria on October 18, 1879. Realizing that the obelisk was really going to be removed, the people of Alexandria began to agitate against it. "Violently abusive articles were published in the newspapers," Gorringe reported, "meetings were held, and petitions to the Khedive were circulated for signature." Gorringe was hissed at in the streets. Realizing he had a serious problem, he and Schroeder went to Cairo to see the khedive and returned with a letter ordering the local governor to turn the obelisk over to them and to give as much assistance as he had given the British two years earlier. To emphasize that the obelisk was now an American possession, Gorringe had an American flag displayed on the obelisk to emphasize that it was American property.

On October 29 work began excavating the base and steps beneath the obelisk and by November 6, 1,730 cubic yards had been removed—entirely by human effort—and dumped in the sea nearby. The stone was sheathed in planking to protect it and on November 11, the machinery for turning the obelisk arrived and was set up atop a masonry foundation.

The trunnion plates were then attached to the obelisk at its center of gravity and a stack of timber was erected to catch the obelisk if there was a mishap. On December 2, the obelisk was raised from the pedestal using hydraulic jacks and the first attempt to turn it was made. It failed, however, as the obelisk bound against the top of one of the metal crabs that Roman engineers had used to stabilize it two thousand years earlier. Many feared that the obelisk would crash, but Gorringe had the crabs removed and was ready to try again.

Four days later, in the presence of the governor and a large crowd, a second attempt was made. As Gorringe wrote,

> the word was given to slack the tackles. A large crowd of Greeks, Italians, and other Europeans had gathered in the vicinity, and occupied every available spot from which the movement could be seen. While we were waiting for the Governor, the crowd was noisy and at times unruly. . . . But at the instant the obelisk began to move there was absolute silence and stillness. As it slowly turned not a sound but the rendering of the ropes around the posts and an occasional creak of the structure could be heard. Immediately following a creak louder than any previous one, the motion was suddenly arrested, then there was a sharp snap—one of the tackles had parted. Instantly the order was given to slack the other tackle rapidly, using it merely to retard the motion and not to arrest it; but the man attending the fall had lost his wits, and instead of slackening, he held it fast and it very soon broke. The obelisk was at that moment about half over; it moved slowly at first and then more and more rapidly, until it struck the

stack of timbers, rebounded twice, and came to rest. . . .
There was intense excitement; many of the [crowd]
had fled precipitously when the obelisk began to
move rapidly; and when it [came to rest] . . . there
arose a prolonged cheer, which was the first
friendly manifestation shown by the
Alexandrians.

It was also about the last. Although the khedive had
ordered that the same assistance that had been given the
British be given to the Americans, it was not forthcoming.
The obelisk was still forty-three feet above the ground and
Gorringe had to use inferior wood to build stacks
surrounding the hydraulic jacks that were to lower the stone

While being lowered in Egypt, "Cleopatra's Needle" crashed into a
stack of wood that broke its fall.

to ground level as the good wood the British had employed was kept in storage.*

The hydraulic jacks would lift the obelisk a few inches and one layer of wood would be removed and the obelisk lowered until it rested on the next layer, the jacks were then lowered and the process repeated, at the rate of about three feet a day. But when it was finally at ground level, the foreign merchants who were in charge of maintaining and cleaning the city streets, claiming that it might damage the water mains, refused permission to transport the obelisk the mile or so it needed to travel to get to where it would be loaded on the ship. Gorringe was forced to build a caisson and float the obelisk around the harbor, a far longer and more hazardous journey.

With the pedestal freed of its burden, it was rolled on cannonballs to one side. Beneath it were found some marked stones and a trowel. Masons promptly claimed that the trowel was evidence of ancient freemasonry, but it was more likely the result of a careless workman's lack of concern for his tools. Gorringe, struck by the possibility however, decided to take the pedestal and the steps that had been beneath it and use them in Central Park. Thus Cleopatra's Needle is the only ancient obelisk removed from its original location to still rest on its original foundation.

* * *

---

* In treeless Egypt, wood was a very expensive commodity.

OBTAINING A SHIP suitable to transport the obelisk was difficult. Gorringe and Schroeder had looked for one in several American ports as well as in England and Scotland without success. In Alexandria they found the *Dessoug*, which had been built in Britain for the Egyptian postal service in 1864 but by 1879 was laid up in the Arsenal, as Alexandria's naval base was called. She was of a suitable size, with a length of 233 feet, a beam of 33 feet, and gross tonnage of 1,367. But as Gorringe noted, "her engines and boilers were known to be in bad condition . . . her hold was filthy, and she had been neglected to a degree that cannot be imagined."

Fearing interference from local ship brokers, Gorringe arranged with the Egyptian postal service to purchase the ship quietly and the first thing the port of Alexandria knew about the transfer was when the Egyptian flag came down from the masthead and the American flag went up. The actual purchaser was the Ocean Steam Navigation Company, controlled by William H. Vanderbilt.

Registering the ship proved to be a problem. A quirk of American law made it impossible for her to be American registered, and Egyptian registry was equally problematic. European registry raised other questions and so Gorringe, ever the brisk, decision-making engineer, decided that "there was no other course than open defiance of law . . . and I determined to make the voyage from Alexandria to New York without registry or nationality."

Once the *Dessoug* had been cleaned and repaired, she was ready to receive the obelisk as soon as the port's dry dock was available. But port officials manufactured delays that lasted for five weeks. Several other ships occupied the dry dock in succession when the work done on them could just as easily have been done elsewhere. Gorringe did manage to obtain permission to move the caisson into the dry dock as it was leaking badly and he thought that "there was danger of its being sunk by accident or design." Once there, the caisson was demolished to ensure that the obelisk could only be loaded on the *Dessoug*.

Loading the pedestal onto the *Dessoug* proved difficult. The hydraulic jacks got it on a barge that was towed over to where the *Dessoug* was moored. But, given that the pedestal weighed fifty tons, no crane available in Alexandria was capable of lifting it onto the ship.

Gorringe arranged for two cranes to be coupled, calculating that together they were capable of lifting fifty-five tons. The pedestal was tied with steel rope but when it was lifted off the barge and the barge moved out of the way so that the stern of the *Dessoug* could receive it, the pedestal began to oscillate. Five of the seven strands of the steel cable had parted. Had the other two parted and the pedestal fallen while over the stern of the *Dessoug*, it would have sunk her in an instant.

Fortunately the two strands held and the pedestal was lowered back onto the barge. The next day, using the *Dessoug's* heaviest anchor chain, the pedestal was safely transferred to the *Dessoug* and secured below.

With the *Dessoug* finally in dry dock, an opening measuring about thirty feet long and twelve feet high was made in her starboard side. It required the removal of seven thousand rivets, sixteen frames, and thirty plates. Sliding the obelisk into the ship, rolling it on cannonballs, went like clockwork and was accomplished in only eight hours. The obelisk was secured amidships and the hole in the side soon repaired and the *Dessoug* left the dry dock, ready to sail.

On June 12, as other ships tooted their steam whistles and dipped their colors in salute, the *Dessoug* set sail for New York. As Gorringe recorded in his book, "to Lieutenant Schroeder and myself the open sea, with the

Loading "Cleopatra's Needle" aboard the *Dessoug* in Alexandria, Egypt.

comparative rest and relief that it brought, was acceptable and enjoyable beyond expression."

Ten days later, the Dessoug dropped anchor off Gibraltar, where they had arranged to take on coal. The boilers, despite having been supposedly fixed in Alexandria, were leaking badly and three days were needed to repair them. Meanwhile many people came to see the obelisk (although it was covered in planking), including the governor, Lord Napier of Magdala.

Four days after leaving Gibraltar, the *Dessoug* sailed through the Azores. But after another six days, when only 1,500 miles from New York, the crankshaft snapped and the *Dessoug* wallowed to a stop. Fortunately there were spare parts aboard and after six days of using only the auxiliary sails, the *Dessoug* resumed her course for New York. The ship soon encountered a gale and Gorringe was pleased to see that "the behavior of the vessel was exceptionally good, as far as her motion was concerned. . . . Very close watch was kept of the obelisk and its fastenings, but not the least motion was detected in anything connected with them."*

Finally, on July 19, 1880, the *Dessoug* picked up a New York harbor pilot and then anchored off Staten Island early on July 20.

* * *

---

* Had the obelisk or its pedestal shifted to any significant degree during the trip, it would, almost certainly, have sunk the *Dessoug* nearly instantly, quite possibly taking everyone with it. It was not unknown in the nineteenth century, before wireless telegraphy began, for ships to simply vanish in mid-Atlantic without a trace. If that had happened, one of the great, enduring mysteries of the nineteenth century would have been about what had happened to Cleopatra's Needle.

WHERE TO SITE the obelisk had been an issue in 1879, before the obelisk had even left Egypt. Many thought that it should be put in a place of great prominence, such as Union Square or Grand Army Plaza, at the southeast corner of Central Park, where later the magnificent gilded statue of General Sherman by Augustus Saint-Gaudens would stand. But the nexus between the trustees of the Metropolitan Museum of Art and the commissioners of Central Park assured that it would be placed in Central Park, on Graywacke Knoll, one of the highest points in Manhattan and just west of the newly opened permanent home of the museum.*

The park commissioners wanted the obelisk in their domain and the museum trustees wanted to assure that it would attract people to the neighborhood and thus to the museum, which was considered far uptown in 1880. Indeed, the area was still only half developed, with unconnected rows of new brownstone townhouses amid fields, orchards, pigpens, chicken coops, and old farmhouses.

They were right to regard the obelisk as a great draw. Almost from the instant that the ship moored off Twenty-third Street in the Hudson River a few days after arriving in New York, it was met by a steady stream of visitors, even though the obelisk was still encased in its protective planking in the gloom of the hold. At the end of July the

---

*The original building, designed by Calvert Vaux—who had been central to the design of Central Park itself—and Jacob Wrey Mould, is nearly invisible today behind the no fewer than twenty additions that have engulfed it.

Dessoug moved to a wharf at the end of Fifty-first Street and prepared to discharge the pedestal, steps, foundation, and erecting machinery.

Gorringe borrowed a derrick from the city and, as he wrote, "the pedestal was lifted out of the steamer and landed on the dock by the derrick with an ease and rapidity that contrasted strangely with its embarkation in Alexandria."

Only one vehicle in New York could, with modifications, move a fifty-ton stone through the streets of the city. The stone was slung on chains between the huge wheels and the truck was pulled by sixteen pairs of huge, powerful, draft horses. The wheels would have to be started with the help of hydraulic jacks and then the horses would proceed at a slow trot, at least until the wheels sank into the pavement from the weight. If they sank more than nine inches, which was the clearance of the stone, the stone had to be unslung, the wheels raised and placed on timber until they could move clear. When the stone reached the park at Eighty-second Street, it was transferred to greased skids and hauled the rest of the way using capstans.

Once Graywacke Knoll* had been prepared, the foundation and steps taken from Alexandria were reassembled on it and time capsules were placed in the spaces between

---

*The name is somewhat mysterious as graywacke is a kind of sandstone, but the knoll itself is an outcropping of Manhattan's famous schist, a type of metamorphic rock.

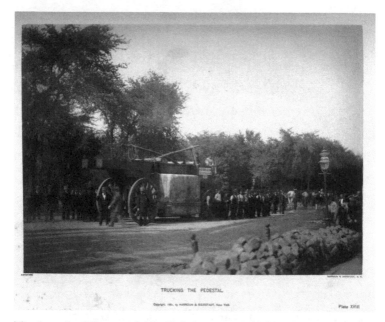

TRUCKING THE PEDESTAL

Plate XVIII

The base for "Cleopatra's Needle" alone weighed fifty tons, here being moved to the chosen location in Central Park.

the stones. They contained everything from the 1870 federal census to a selection of screws and assorted hardware, a hydraulic pump, Masonic paraphernalia, and a tourist guide to Egypt.*

Some nine thousand Freemasons marched up Fifth Avenue for the solemn ceremony of laying the cornerstone, complete with marching bands. The pedestal was then swung into position and the turning machinery brought

---

*Unless catastrophe strikes, the time capsules placed in the bases of the various obelisks will likely remain unopened for eternity as they cannot be accessed without moving the obelisk and pedestal.

back from Alexandria was reassembled, ready to receive the obelisk.

Where to land the obelisk on Manhattan was a problem. The east side of the island, with its low-lying shore, would have been more convenient and closer to Graywacke Knoll, but the East River that runs along Manhattan's eastern shore is not in fact a river at all. It is a tidal race, connecting Long Island Sound with New York Harbor. As those two bodies of water reach high tide at different times, the current racing between them can reach eight knots, which would have hugely complicated the task of transferring 220 tons of granite from barge to land. So it would have to be landed on the west side of Manhattan, but much of the upper west side banks steeply to the Hudson River.* The only possible landing place was at Ninety-sixth Street.

The owner of the only suitable dry dock wanted to charge exorbitantly for its use, so Gorringe arranged for the disembarkation to be on Staten Island, using a marine railway, up which ships were hauled for painting and repairs less extensive than those that would have required a dry dock.

Once the *Dessoug* had been hauled up out of the water, the first rivets were removed from her side on August 22 and two weeks later the obelisk was hauled out of the *Dessoug* on cannonballs onto heavy timbers positioned on

---

* The Hudson River, like the East River, is not a river. It is an estuary, an arm of the sea. It is sea level, and tidal, as far north as Albany.

pilings. Between the timbers were two pontoons filled with water.

On September 16, the *Dessoug* repaired and out of the way, the pontoons were pumped out at low tide. As the tide came in, the pontoons, now filled with air, lifted the obelisk and its timbers until they floated free of the pilings and could be towed out of the slip. A few hours later, at Ninety-sixth Street, the procedure was reversed and as the tide fell, the obelisk finally reached Manhattan.

The tracks of the Hudson River Railroad (a Vander-bilt property) ran along the shoreline* and needed to be crossed quickly to minimize the amount of time when trains would have to be halted. The longest stretch, during daylight, without trains passing was an hour and a half, about noon. Gorringe designed a bridge for getting the obelisk across the tracks and, rolling on cannonballs in channels, it cleared the tracks in one hour and twenty minutes. Only a freight train was held up, and for less than half an hour.

But getting the obelisk across the tracks revealed that the plan of using cannonballs in wooden channels wouldn't work to get the obelisk to Central Park. The enormous weight of the obelisk kept cracking the channels and there was no way to reinforce them. Gorringe would have to come up with another plan.

He built a cradle, consisting of wooden beams joined by struts in which the obelisk rested. Ahead of it on the

---

* They still do, but now mostly underground.

"Cleopatra's Needle" being transported from a dock on the Hudson River, across railroad tracks, toward Central Park.

cradle was a pile-driving engine with a winch. Beams were also used for the "tracks," with rollers in roll boxes sandwiched between the cradle and the tracks. Ahead, a stationary block was anchored firmly in the roadway. The *Dessoug*'s heavy anchor chain was attached to it, and the engine on the cradle wound the chain around the winch drum, moving itself and the obelisk slowly forward.

It was very slow going. Before each movement, the ground had to be graded, the block anchored, the heavy beams moved forward, and the anchor chain, which itself weighed tons, unwound and hauled forward to the block. The system was first used on September 30, and it worked, but delays were caused by bad weather and the difficulty in finding suitable workmen. Also the hill up to Broadway is one of the steepest in Manhattan. As a result, the obelisk reached Broadway only on October 27.

The obelisk then had to be turned ninety degrees south in order to go down Broadway to Eighty-sixth Street, where it would use the Eighty-sixth Street transverse to cross the park. That first turn, onto Broadway, took an agonizing six days to accomplish. Gorringe, ever the problem-solving engineer, designed what might be called an obelisk-turning device and the next ninety-degree turn, at Eighty-sixth Street, took only four hours.

All through November and December, as the season turned into one of the worst New York winters of the nineteenth century, Cleopatra's Needle inched toward its final destination on Graywacke Knoll. As Gorringe wrote,

> to add to the difficulties of this part of the work, intensely cold weather alternated with heavy falls of snow, and the picked men gave out one by one from attacks of rheumatism and other effects of exposure. The time occupied in moving the obelisk through the transverse road was nineteen days. Work was carried on continuously night and day by two gangs, relieving each other at six o'clock morning and evening. I made a point to spend six hours of each day and five hours of each night personally superintending the work.

New York entrepreneurs, predictably, began exploiting the mounting obelisk fever that was gripping the city. A candy stand followed the obelisk along its route, selling sweets to the crowds of onlookers. Restaurants began selling a new drink, an "obbylish," and a candy called Cleopatra Dates was sold in an obelisk-shaped box. A guard had to be posted to prevent people, often arriving with hammers and chisels, from attacking the obelisk to obtain souvenirs.

On December 16 it reached Fifth Avenue and began the four-block trip down the avenue to where it made its last turn, into Central Park and onto a purpose-built trestle. Finally, it reached Graywacke Knoll on January 5, 1881. Thanks to the trestle, the obelisk's center of gravity could be positioned directly above the pedestal and foundation.

The trip from the Hudson River and Ninety-sixth Street to Graywacke Knoll had taken 112 days, the obelisk moving, on average, an almost imperceptible five feet an hour.

On January 20, 1881, the turning structure was in place and the trunnion plates grasped the obelisk at the center of gravity. That night Gorringe and a picked crew met at the site at midnight to test the machinery. As the New York *World*, whose proprietor William Henry Hurlbert had been central to the obelisk project, reported:

Bonfires had been built on each side and the scene was most weird and picturesque as the huge mass of 220 tons swung majestically from the horizontal to the vertical position. A large and merry party returning home in sleighs on the drive past the site were attracted by the fires and the sound of voices and halted to witness the experiment. They rose in their sleighs and cheered lustily as the monolith majestically rose to its position. [Half an hour later,] the fires had all been extinguished, the workmen had left for home, and the obelisk was lying horizontal again on its trunnions as if nothing had happened.

The official erection was scheduled for noon on January 22, despite a winter gale that had swept through the city the day before. Regardless of the snow and cold, at least ten thousand people turned out to see Cleopatra's Needle move for the last time. Secretary of State William Evarts and Secretary of the Navy Nathan Goff, Jr., were on hand and at noon, Gorringe gave the signal to begin the operation.

The crowd watched in eerie silence as the great stone began to move toward the vertical. Gorringe signaled for the operation to stop at the halfway point so that a photograph could be taken. This broke the spell and the crowd began to cheer as the operation resumed. In five minutes the obelisk rested once more on its pedestal and Gorringe could relax.

"It was to me," he wrote, "an inexpressible relief to feel that my work was complete, and that no accident or incident had happened that would make my countrymen regret that I had been intrusted with the work of removing and re-erecting in their metropolis one of the most famous monuments of the Old World."

"Cleopatra's Needle" in Central Park today, close to the Metropolitan Museum.

New bronze crabs, cast to replace the ones the Romans had made to stabilize the obelisk, were soon in place and Gorringe calculated that a force capable of lifting seventy-eight tons, applied to the obelisk's center of gravity, would be needed to topple it. The maximum force of hurricane winds would be no more than enough to lift five tons. "It would require an exceptionally severe earthquake," Gorringe wrote, "one that would leave very few buildings in New York standing, to render the obelisk unstable."

All that was left was the ceremony and oratory so beloved of Victorians, turning the obelisk over to the Metropolitan Museum of Art. That was held in the museum's Great Hall a month later, on George Washington's birthday. Henry G. Stebbins was unable to attend because of a severe cold* but his speech was read out for him. This "artistic memorial," he said, "now fitly looks on the beginning of what I trust will become a great museum of art. . . . I hope that the successful placing of this interesting monument in relation to the future national gallery of America will encourage our wealthy citizens to enlarge the Art Museum and to fill it with those treasures which so greatly increase the attractions of the metropolis."†

---

* Stebbins would die the following December.

† Stebbins's hope was to be more than fulfilled. Today the Metropolitan Museum of Art is the greatest single repository of art in the world, equaled, perhaps, only by the Louvre.

CHAPTER EIGHT

Into the Twenty-first Century

WHILE THE WASHINGTON Monument had been dedicated, it was not yet ready to be officially opened to the
public, although it was informally open. Metal stair treads
and landings had to replace the temporary wooden ones.
By the time that was done, in September 1886, more than
ten thousand people had already climbed the five hundred
feet to the top. The freight hoist that had been used to lift
stone was replaced with a proper metal passenger elevator
car by the end of 1886. Once the elevator was installed, the
number of visitors reached fifty thousand a month.

The windows in the pyramidion had been the means of
hanging the scaffolding that surrounded the pyramidion as
the capstone was placed. The scaffolding had to be removed

and the windows fitted. Electric lighting—cutting-edge technology at a time when gaslight and kerosene still overwhelmingly predominated—was installed. Electricity would not be installed in the White House until 1891.

The biggest unfinished part of the project was the surrounding grounds. Much of the foundation was visible and the question was how to landscape the area immediately surrounding the monument. One proposal was to build a large paved terrace, surrounded with a retaining wall. But that would have cost more than half a million dollars and Congress, never enthusiastic about paying for the monument at all, balked at the price.

The alternative was to bring in landfill and smooth out the contours of the hill on which the monument stands, covering the foundation in the process. Thus the Washington Monument is a rarity among obelisks: It does not stand on a visible base but seems instead to just emerge from the earth.

The monument was officially opened to the public in 1888.

Soon the lightning protection system that Thomas Casey had designed was found to be inadequate. He had been confident that the aluminum cap at the top of the Washington Monument, connected to the metal columns that held the elevator—which, in turn, was grounded—would be all the lightning protection that the monument needed. Aluminum was known to be an even better conductor of electricity than copper (indeed it is better than all other metals except silver).

But only four months after the main construction ended, he was proved wrong. On Friday, June 5, 1885, the monument was struck by lightning and damaged. As the *New York Times* reported,

> the injury, which can be seen with a strong glass, appears to be a seam across one block of marble in the course immediately below the capstone. A small fragment of the capstone, on the northeast angle of the pyramid, was also detached. The damage is considered trifling, but the fear that in a severer storm the shaft may be shattered has led to the employment of experts to suggest precautionary measures. The examination . . . led them to conclude that the apparatus for carrying off electricity inside the monument was all that could be desired; in fact, it was almost too good, the trouble being an insufficient connection with the outside. The committee will make a report in writing as to the necessary changes, and will probably recommend that holes be drilled at different places in the thin roof stones, through which conductors may pass to the outside from the iron rod conductors in the interior, thus giving other points for the lightning to strike besides the aluminum tip.

Casey didn't wait for the report. He ordered four copper rods, three quarters of an inch thick, to run from the interior copper rods that connected to the iron elevator supports to each face of the pyramidion. From the face they would branch out into seven different terminals, giving the lightning a total of twenty-nine places to strike and be conveyed safely to the ground. Because of the monument's height, these extra lightning rods were invisible from the ground.

Lightning does as it pleases, and no structure can be made completely safe from it. On July 13, 1899, lightning hit the monument and instead of traveling to the ground, it left the northwest iron column at the fifty-foot level and struck the floor plates of the elevator and exploded. From there it

Attaching a new lightning rod to the tip of the Washington Monument in 1934.

made its way to the engine room and burned out the telephone that connected the engine room to the boiler house.

Less than a year later a man was leaning against one of the iron columns when lightning hit the monument and, as the *New York Times* reported he received "quite a heavy shock of electricity in his shoulder and arm." Two men at the top of the monument thought the lightning entered through one of the windows, blinding them temporarily.

The lightning protection system has been modified several times since, including during the 1934 and 1998 restoration projects, and there have been no reports of its failure in recent decades.

INEVITABLY, STUNTS INVOLVING the Washington Monument began soon after its completion. In 1908, Washington Senators catcher Gabby Street, remembered in baseball history from his managing days as "the Old Sarge," caught a baseball thrown from one of the windows at the top of the monument by a journalist named Preston Gibson. Gibson threw a ball twelve times and Street tried to catch four of them, finally succeeding on the fourth try. It was a considerable feat, seeing as he couldn't even see the ball until it was about halfway down.

Asked how it felt to catch the ball, Street replied, "It didn't strike with terrific force, as one might expect . . . just about like stopping a fast one from a pitcher with plenty of steam." Street knew what he was talking about regarding pitchers with steam as he caught for and mentored legendary pitcher Walter Johnson, nicknamed "the Big Train" for his extraordinary fastball. He was among the first five inductees into the Baseball Hall of Fame along with Babe Ruth, Honus Wagner, Ty Cobb, and Christy Mathewson.*

Other things would be, from time to time, thrown out the windows, including a marble and an orange, both of which injured people on the ground. In 1926, bars were put across the windows after three suicides. The windows were sealed after air-conditioning was installed.

FOR THIRTY-FIVE YEARS, the monument stood by itself unadorned by anything. Then, on Washington's birthday in 1920, forty-eight wooden flag poles were temporarily erected in a circle around the monument and American flags were raised, one for each state in the union at the time. The poles were lowered and stored when not in use. Soon the flags were also flying on July 4, Memorial Day, and on special occasions such as Victory in Europe and Victory over Japan days as well as Washington's birthday.

In 1958, fifty twenty-five-foot aluminum poles were arrayed in a circle around the monument 260 feet in

---

* Street, a journeyman player, never came close to getting into the Hall of Fame, but he holds one, odd baseball record. His career as a player ended in 1912. But, while managing the St. Louis Cardinals in 1931 (they won the World Series that year), he played in one game. The nineteen-year interval between major-league games remains a record, as it probably will forever.

diameter. Although Alaska and Hawaii were not yet in the union, their accession to it was anticipated. On Washington's birthday that year, forty-eight flags were flown, and they have flown every day since. A forty-ninth flag was added on July 4, 1959, as Alaska entered the union, and a fiftieth the following year when Hawaii joined.* The flags, at first, were lowered at night, but since July 4, 1971, they have been illuminated and flown twenty-four hours a day. In 2004 the circle was reduced to 240 feet in diameter.

In 1930 the monument was deemed a hazard to nighttime flying and lights, buried in the ground, were installed around the monument to light its lower portion. To illuminate the upper portion, a searchlight had already been mounted on the Navy Building, a "temporary" structure on the Mall that had been built in 1918 during World War One. It was finally torn down in 1970.†

By this time, the monument was showing its age. Fifty years of wind, sun, rain, and lightning had both dirtied and damaged the structure. In 1934 it was decided to erect what was then the world's tallest scaffolding to both assess the damage and repair it as necessary. The cost was estimated at about one hundred thousand dollars, roughly a million in today's money.

---

* States are admitted by act of Congress and a new star is added to the flag on the following July Fourth.
† Today there is a red navigation light blinking atop the monument. The District of Columbia is a no-fly zone for general aviation aircraft but scheduled air traffic often flies quite close to the monument as it approaches Reagan National Airport.

Fifty state flags surround the Washington Monument.

The scaffolding was made of metal, then unusual for scaffolding, as a precaution against fire. It had platforms every seven feet and when the scaffolding reached 150 feet, a little more than one quarter the way up, work was scheduled to begin.

Even before the scaffolding was completed the damage was discovered to be more extensive than originally thought. Rain had penetrated in many places eroding the mortar between the stones, and 48,046 linear feet of the mortar needed to be replaced. However, the missing mortar was not the only problem.

On November 5, 1934, the Associated Press reported on the monument's condition:

> A half century's battering by the elements has cracked and strained the Washington Monument to such an extent that whole blocks of marble must be pried from its face and replaced.
>
> The monument is safe, but the National Park Service has found that damaged marble slabs must be removed. Some of them have been cracked all the way through. Engineers say this is due to the swaying of the 555-foot shaft. Lightning has split some blocks in several directions and the weight of the structure itself has shattered others. The monument sways several inches in a high wind. Even the sun moves it. The expansion of the shaft caused by the sun's shining with full strength on the south side has made the giant obelisk move as much as two and five-eighth inches toward the north.*

By the 1990s, the problems of aging had recurred. "It leaks like a sieve," one National Park Service official

---

* In fact, it does not sway significantly. Tall steel buildings do sway slightly (indeed are designed to), but stone doesn't flex, even in high winds. Nor does sunlight cause the monument to flex. Stone, unlike steel, has a very low coefficient of expansion and the white marble facing reflects much of the sun's energy.

said. In 1996 survey work began to detail what restoration was needed and planning began on a new air-conditioning system and elevator machinery as well as improved heat and ventilation. The following year Secretary of the Interior Bruce Babbitt announced that corporations, showing more generosity than American citizens had shown a hundred and forty years earlier, had raised five million dollars to repair the monument. Among the sponsors were Target, Procter & Gamble, Coca-Cola, Eastman Kodak, and the country and western singer Garth Brooks.

In January 1998, the monument closed for several months while the interior work was done. When it was completed the exterior work began with the erection of a scaffolding designed by the distinguished architect Michael Graves. It was covered with a transparent fabric that had blue lines reminiscent of the stone and mortar pattern of the monument itself. This allowed people to watch the work in progress. General Electric supplied the lighting system that illuminated the new fabric skin at night. The scaffolding was thought so beautiful that a petition even circulated asking that it be made a permanent part of the monument.

As is usual with government projects, the restoration took longer than expected and cost more than estimated, finally coming in at $10.5 million. Because the stairs had been closed to the public since the 1970s, the new elevator cab had glass panels so that the passengers could see the commemorative stones set in the interior wall. The monument finally reopened for good on Washington's birthday, 2002.

But in 2004, in the wake of 9/11, it closed again, this time for a fifteen-million-dollar security upgrade as well as new landscaping. It reopened on April 1, 2005.

THE VULNERABILITY OF the monument to terrorism had already been demonstrated. At nine twenty A.M. on December 8, 1982, a man drove a truck up to the entrance, blocking it. The driver told tourists that he had a bomb, specifically a thousand pounds of dynamite. The Park Police quickly moved the tourists away, but there were seven tourists and two Park Service employees in the monument. For safety, they moved to the observation level at the top of the monument.

Emergency equipment, including an armored vehicle, fire trucks, and ambulances arrived, along with police and what the *New York Times* described as "heavily armed members of a special weapons team."

The commerce and agriculture departments were evacuated from their nearby office buildings and the Smithsonian's National Museum of American History was closed for the day. At the White House, several hundred yards away, a luncheon meeting of President Ronald Reagan scheduled for the State Dining Room was moved, for fear that an explosion might break the windows. First Lady Nancy Reagan was asked to avoid the south-facing windows.

The man, later identified as Norman David Mayer, age sixty-six, of Miami, Florida, demanded that "the first order of business on every agenda of every organization" be the banning of nuclear weapons. His truck had a sign saying I PRIORITY: BAN NUCLEAR WEAPONS. Mayer, dressed in a padded blue jumpsuit and a bubble helmet with a dark visor, spent the day pacing around the monument, carrying a backpack with an antenna sticking out of it. He claimed to be able to detonate the bomb remotely.

He demanded that a negotiator, a journalist without dependents, be appointed and Steve Komarow of the Associated Press volunteered. He spoke to Mayer several times and at two o'clock, Mayer agreed to let the nine people trapped in the monument leave.

The closed streets caused massive traffic jams in the city and hundreds came out to see the drama but were kept well back from the scene.

Finally, at about seven thirty that evening, Mayer got into the truck and tried to drive away. The authorities had already decided that if Mayer attempted to leave, they would shoot to prevent him from doing so. That risked an explosion of the dynamite, but they felt that it was far better to have the truck explode in the wide open space of the Mall than in the narrow streets of Washington.

Snipers fired several shots at the vehicle and it turned over. Moving cautiously, the police took forty-five minutes to remove Mayer, fatally wounded with a bullet through the head, from the overturned van. There was no dynamite in the truck nor in the monument, which was subjected to a four-hour search.

Could a thousand pounds of dynamite have brought down the Washington Monument? Almost certainly not. In World War Two, a thousand-pound bomb was dubbed a "blockbuster" because it was large enough to destroy an entire city block. But the walls of the monument, designed to sustain the enormous weight of the structure, are fully fifteen feet thick at the base and made of solid granite. Much of the marble facing would surely have been destroyed but the structure itself would have survived with only that superficial damage.

THE ARRIVAL OF the twentieth century did not mean that the age of the obelisk was over. The shape continues both to fascinate and to appeal to those who want to demonstrate their power, just as Thutmose III did 3,500 years earlier.

In 1928, Czechoslovakia, established by the treaty of Versailles following World War One out of the ruins of the Hapsburg Empire, wanted to celebrate its tenth anniversary as an independent state. It commissioned an obelisk, to be quarried from a single piece of granite. It would have been one of the largest monolithic obelisks ever made. Unfortunately, while being transported to Prague where it was to be erected outside Saint Vitus Cathedral in the Prague Castle complex, the obelisk rolled down an embankment and broke in two. Only the top half could be salvaged and it stands today, still an impressive fifty-five feet high, next to the cathedral.

In 1936, the city of Buenos Aires celebrated its four hundredth anniversary by building an obelisk. Located at the intersection of two of the city's main roads, Avenida Corrientes and Avenida Nueve de Julio,* at 220 feet high it can be seen from many parts of the largely flat city.

It was built in the remarkably short time of two months, using poured concrete instead of stone, and has

The obelisk in Buenos Aires, Argentina.

---

* The Ninth of July is Argentina's independence day. The avenue itself, the Champs Élysées of Buenos Aires, is the widest in the world, with no fewer than fourteen lanes of traffic and eight more in flanking side streets.

been a symbol of the city ever since, often subjected to graffiti, political theater, and even political threats. In 1975 a sign was hung on the Obelisco that said, "*EL SILENCIO ES SALUD*," "Silence is Health." While it was, ostensibly, a warning against Buenos Aires's notoriously noisy traffic, most Porteños, as the people of Buenos Aires are called, took it as a political warning from the increasingly authoritarian government of Isabel Perón.

The next year the army seized control and, in what came to be called *La Noche de los Lápices* ("the Night of the Pencils"), many young people were kidnapped and disappeared. The army dictatorship fell with the end of the Falklands War in 1982 and in 2006, the thirtieth anniversary of that terrible night was commemorated by decorating the Obelisco as a pencil. The previous year, to celebrate AIDS Awareness Day, it had been wrapped in a giant pink condom.

In 1936, to celebrate the renaming of the capital city of the Dominican Republic after himself, the dictator of the country, Rafael Trujillo, ordered the erection of an obelisk, 137 feet in height, along the shore of the city. At the dedication ceremony, the obelisk was said to mirror Trujillo's "superior natural gifts." Trujillo was assassinated in 1961 and in 1997 the obelisk was decorated with a mural that celebrates the three Mirabal sisters, whose opposition to Trujillo brought about their own deaths in 1960 but also the end of the Trujillo regime the following year.

In the 1960s the American abstract expressionist Barnett Newman created a sculpture called *Broken Obelisk*. Weighing three tons, it is fabricated of steel and shows a pyramid above

Pyramidic sculpture by Barnett Newman. Nationalgalerie, Staatliche Museen, Berlin, Germany.

whose apex an upside-down broken obelisk teeters, or at least appears to, as the contact point is only a few centimeters across. There are several multiples of this sculpture, including at the Museum of Modern Art in New York, the Rothko Chapel in Houston; the Storm King Art Center in New Windsor, N.Y.; the University of Washington in Seattle, and the Berlin State Museums in Germany.

* * *

IN 1890, TWO years after the Washington Monument's official opening, the editor of Baedeker's guide to the United States described the monument as "one of the noblest monuments ever raised to mortal man. When gleaming in the westering sun, like a slender, tapering sky-pointing finger of gold, no finer index can be imagined to direct the gazer to the record of a glorious history."

Since then the Washington Monument has served as a backdrop for history itself as the once sleepy southern town that surrounds it evolved into the capital of the free world.

Because it is visible from so much of the city, it has appeared in everything from fashion shows to inaugurations. In 1939 Marian Anderson faced the monument as she sang from the steps of the Lincoln Memorial in the very early days of the civil rights movement. Martin Luther King Jr. likewise looked out on the monument as that movement approached its climax twenty-four years later, in August 1963.

In 1945 the relighting of the monument signaled the end of wartime restrictions. In the 1960s hippies frolicked naked in its shadow and protestors demanded an end to the Vietnam War. In 1976 it was the centerpiece of a massive fireworks display celebrating the Bicentennial. In the 1980s the AIDS quilt was laid out before it, recording the names of the thousands who had died from that terrible disease.

Silent and imperturbable as always, the Washington Monument will doubtless witness much more history as it continues to stand at the symbolic epicenter of the extraordinary country that George Washington, more than any other single person, had made possible.

The Washington Monument seen from the Lincoln Memorial, 1992.

ACKNOWLEDGMENTS

As always, I owe much thanks to my editor, George Gibson, especially for his patience, which exceeded even my procrastination. His skillful editing, when I finally delivered the manuscript, much improved it.

I would also like to thank my agent, Katinka Matson, of Brockman, Inc.

The Ruth Keeler Memorial Library in North Salem, New York, and the Union Club library in New York City were both invaluable.

I would also like to thank Janet McDonald for her excellent copyediting and Megha Jain for her equally excellent proofreading. They both saved me from many errors, solecisms, and typos.

BIBLIOGRAPHY

Abbot, Henry L. "Memoir of Thomas Lincoln Casey, 1831–1896."
Washington, D.C.: National Academy of Sciences, 1897.

Allen, Thomas B. *The Washington Monument: It Stands for All.* New
York: Discovery Books, 2000.

Binczewski, George J. "The Point of a Monument: A History of the
Aluminum Cap of the Washington Monument." *JOM* (a
publication of the Minerals, Metals, and Materials Society):
November 1995.

Brier, Bob. *Egyptomania: Our Three Thousand Year Obsession with the
Land of the Pharaohs.* New York: Palgrave MacMillan, 2013.

Budge, E. A. Wallis. *Cleopatra's Needles and Other Egyptian Obelisks.*
New York: Dover Publications, 1990. A reprint of the 1926
edition.

Crofts, Daniel W., A Secession Crisis Enigma: William H. Hurlbert and "The Diary of a Public Man. Baton Rouge, La.:
Lousiana State University Press, 2010.

Curran, Brian A. Anthony Grafton, Pamela O. Long, and Benjamin
Weiss. *Obelisk: A History.* Cambridge, Mass.: Burndy Library,
2009.

D'Alton, Martina. *The New York Obelisk, or How Cleopatra's Needle
Came to New York and What Happened When It Got Here.* New
York: Metropolitan Museum of Art/Abrams, 1993.

The Dedication of the Washington National Monument. Washington,
D.C.: Government Printing Office, 1885.

Dibner, Bern. *Moving the Obelisks: A Chapter in Engineering History
in which the Vatican Obelisk in Rome in 1586 was Moved by*

Muscle Power, and a Study of More Recent Moves. Cambridge, Mass.: M.I.T. Press, 1950.

Gorringe, Henry H. *Egyptian Obelisks.* London: John Nimmo, 1885.

Harvey, Frederick. *History of the Washington National Monument and of the Washington National Monument Society.* Washington, D.C.: 1902.

Paine, Lincoln. *The Sea and Civilization: A Maritime History of the World.* New York: Knopf, 2013.

Romer, John. *A History of Ancient Egypt: From the First Farmers to the Great Pyramid.* New York: St. Martin's Press, 2012.

Sorek, Susan. *The Emperors' Needles: Egyptian Obelisks and Rome.* Exeter, England: Bristol Phoenix Press, 2010.

ILLUSTRATION CREDITS

Library of Congress: Frontispiece, Theodor Horydczak Collection; Pages 146, 182

National Park Service: Pages 2, 4, 26, 58, 198

Smithsonian American Art Museum: Page 20, Horatio Greenough, 1910.10.3 Transfer from the U.S. Capitol

New-York Historical Society: Page 172, William H. Vanderbilt, portrait; from PR052 (Portrait File), box 140; neg #59021, Page 193, Cleopatra's Needle, Central Park, E. Bierstadt, 1881; PR020 (Geographic File), Box 49, Folder Statuary–Obelisk; neg #80189d

Librairie Francaise: Page 174

Science Museum, UK: Page 182

The Barnett Newman Foundation: Pg. 210 © 2015 The Barnett Newman Foundation, New York/Artists Rights Society (ARS), New York; bpk, Berlin/Nationalgalerie, Staatliche Museen, Berlin, Germany/Roman Maerz/Art Resource, NY

All other images are in public domain.

INDEX

Page numbers in *italics* denote illustrations or figures. The letter n following a page number indicates a footnote.

A NOTE ON THE AUTHOR

JOHN STEELE GORDON is one of America's leading historians, especially in the realm of business and financial history. He is the author of *The Scarlet Woman of Wall Street*, *Hamilton's Blessing*, *A Thread Across the Ocean*, *An Empire of Wealth*, and *The Great Game*. He has written for *Forbes*, *Worth*, the *New York Times*, and the *Washington Post*, and his op-eds appear regularly in the *Wall Street Journal*. He writes "The Long View" column for *Barron's*. John Steele Gordon lives in North Salem, New York.